D0837054

BLIMP PILOT TERRORIZES AKRON

AND OTHER HOT AIR
FROM COLUMNIST

BOB DYER

BLIMP PILOT TERRORIZES AKRON

AND OTHER HOT AIR
FROM COLUMNIST

BOB DYER

GRAY & COMPANY, PUBLISHERS

CLEVELAND

Gray & Company, Publishers
www.grayco.com

ISBN: 978-1-938441-48-6

Printed in the U.S.A.

1

My best ideas come from you, the readers of the Akron Beacon Journal. So this book belongs to you.

Well, only if you've already bought it. I just meant that figuratively. You still have to pay for this thing, because I did all the typing.

The reason I still love what I do after more than a quarter-century is my interaction with readers, who inspire me, make me smile, make me angry, laugh at my jokes (sometimes) and tell me lots of things I didn't know. Even the people who hate the stuff I write have provided inspiration—for additional stuff they hated.

Thanks also to the colleagues who shower me with tips, the editors who mostly leave me alone (but sometimes save me from myself) and, especially, the Beacon Journal's copy editors, who toil in complete obscurity, at night, while the reporters and columnists get all the public attention. The folks on the copy desk are true journalists who care only about getting things right. Well, that and collecting those enormous paychecks.

Special thanks go to former Beacon Journal publisher John Dotson. In a front-page story in the New York Times on June 29, 2000, a Times reporter wrote: "Mr. Dotson . . . characterized Mr. Dyer's columns as generally too sarcastic and negative."

That assessment inspired me to be a lot less negative and a lot less sarcastic.

Yeah, right.

Bob Dyer

Contents

Weird Scenes Inside the Gold Mine

The Sporting Life

Readers Rite Good

The Bigger Picture

POLITICALLY INCORRECT

Stow Photo Op Creates Roadblock

If you wanted to find a single story that illustrates everything that's wrong with 21st-century America, you could do a lot worse than this.

The Ohio Department of Transportation told me on Jan. 26 that all of the work on the new interchange for state Route 8 on the Hudson-Stow border had been completed. The only thing left to do, I was told, was for the city of Stow to move the orange cones and open it up.

Well, Stow didn't open it that week.

Or the next.

And Stow won't open it this week.

Or next.

Stow will open it on the afternoon of Feb. 26.

Why? Because Stow wanted to wait until it could get a bunch of politicians together for a ribbon-cutting ceremony, and Feb. 26 was the first time all of their schedules meshed.

I kid thee not.

The public will be deprived of the use of a $6.2 million project for 31 days simply to create a photo op.

Even worse, Stow's mayor, Karen Fritschel, doesn't see anything wrong with that.

"We've had a lot of people who have facilitated the building of the Seasons Road interchange," she says, "and we wanted to invite those people to the grand opening, because we received federal funding from Congressman [Steve] LaTourette and Senator [George] Voinovich, among some others, and we wanted to recognize them.

"That's why we were waiting. We had to have time to get out the invitations and so forth.

"We had to also have all three mayors—Cuyahoga Falls, Stow and Hudson—available for the same date and time."

Do you honestly think the people who have been clamoring for the interchange to open will think a ribbon-cutting is worth waiting an extra month?

"Well, you know, it's been in the works for 25 years, so in looking at the long-range perspective, and in gratitude to the people who made it possible, I think it was," Fritschel says.

Actually, the "people who made it possible" are not the people who will attend the photo op, but the drivers who want to use it— drivers who have paid taxes out the wazoo for the last 25 years for one public project after another.

You know, the people who drag themselves out of bed each morning and drive to work, even when it's gloomy and cold and slushy, and maybe they don't feel too well, or maybe they have a sick kid at home, and they're probably working harder and harder for less and less money, and they're worrying about all kinds of things, and at the end of the day they just want to get home.

If those people encounter a "photo op," it will be at the license bureau, where they will pay 175 percent more for their eye test than they did a year ago.

Those are the people who "made it possible." And they should have been allowed to use this interchange the millisecond it was finished.

Fritschel says she hasn't fielded a single call from someone asking when it would open.

That's probably because most people think ODOT was dictating the opening, not Stow.

My email box started filling up back in November, when eager drivers were eyeing what looked like a finished project. They wanted to know the nature of the holdup.

Initially, the delay was striping the pavement. Work crews couldn't put down their paint in bad weather.

Once the weather broke and the road was painted, a problem arose with the last item on the punch list: The light poles, manu-factured in New York, were delayed by an East Coast snowstorm.

But the poles were erected on Jan. 25, and Ohio Edison hooked them up the next day. The interchange could have opened that after-noon.

I don't know about you, but I'm rooting for a Feb. 26 blizzard.

Feb. 12, 2010

'PC' Push Simply Gets in the Way

Happy Day for People Who are Mothers.

I almost wrote "Happy Mother's Day," but that would have been offensive, because I neglected to note that mothers are, first and foremost, people, just like you and me.

I have come to this realization thanks to a helpful reader who works at a public agency in another county.

The morning after I wrote a 2,500-word story about a dispute among board members at the Autism Family Foundation in Copley—an organization consisting of a family center and a school called "Kids First"—I listened to a voicemail from a woman who identified herself as Dr. Jan Manes.

She further identified herself as the director of education for a developmental disabilities board. And she was more than ready to educate a wayward newspaper writer.

Actually, she seemed to want more than to simply educate. She wanted to make it crystal clear that the writer in question was insensitive and offensive.

Her tone was similar to the tone one might take if one observed a passer-by urinating in one's flower bed.

"I just really cannot believe the article was written not considering, as the school is called, 'Kids First,' " she snarled.

"It should be always stated, 'a child with autism' or 'children with autism.' We do refer to our children as children first, and then the disability, because that's exactly who they are. They are children first.

"It was amazing that not only did you use the term 'autistic kids,' but also those that [sic] were quoted in the paper that [sic] supposedly are associated with a center for children with autism."

Well mea bleeping culpa.

I will henceforth adhere strictly to your secret language rule, because clearly there is an enormous difference between "autistic kids" and "kids with autism." In fact, the unfortunate condition would probably just disappear if we changed the order of the words.

That word order was the sum total of the woman's observations after reading a lengthy story that examined a series of bitter confrontations among the people responsible for the fledgling operation, a falling-out so nasty that it had seemingly threatened to torpedo a noble effort to assist autistic—er, to assist young human beings with the unfortunate-but-manageable condition of autism.

But I have seen the light. I am *heeeeealed,* as they say at Grace Cathedral.

Never again will I ridicule defenseless children by identifying the condition that sets them apart, the condition for which the Autism Center was created, before I note that they are children, rather than, I guess, inanimate objects.

I shall carry this lesson through to all of my writings. For instance, forevermore I will use the term "person who got into an accident" rather than "accident victim," lest we forget that the person being written about—written about only because he/she was involved in an accident—is a person, just like you and me.

And I shall go with "people who play baseball" rather than the flippant term "baseball players," because I now realize they are people, and they surely would prefer to be known first and foremost as people, rather than—*expectorate*—"baseball players."

This is the kind of absurd political correctness that just gets in the way.

To be sure, words have power. Words can heal, and words can wound.

You don't call someone a "retard" or a "ho" or a "[insert your favorite ethnic or racial slur here]." But we should certainly be able to discuss the rapidly growing incidence of autism without having to adhere to a language law dictated by people with good intentions but a tin ear for common sense.

Manes could have criticized me for not taking additional space to write about the remarkable breadth of the spectrum of autism, which includes some high-functioning kids who do so well they graduate from college.

She could have criticized me for not making room to talk about the special techniques teachers and therapists use to bring autistic kids out of their shells.

She could have criticized me for not pointing out that some

doctors believe the huge national increase in autism is caused in large measure by an expanded definition of the disorder.

But don't pick up the phone and insist that using the phrase "autistic kids," rather than "kids with autism," is a horrendous offense.

It is trivia. It is a meaningless distinction that doesn't belong anywhere on the autism agenda.

My caller, as you might assume, has a somewhat different take on this.

When told in a return phone call that I was "astounded" by her complaint, she expressed equal astonishment that I had not already seen the error of my ways.

"Oh, my gosh! Really?"

Really.

"Maybe it's just needing some education for the community and education for the media — being educated in the sense that we should refer to a child with a disability and you look at the child first. They're children. They're not 'autistic' first."

Manes said she felt strongly that her job required educating people like me—felt so strongly that, well, she didn't want her place of employment identified. I was ordered to write only that she has "30-plus years of experience."

After each of us repeated our original arguments three or four different ways, she proclaimed, "I have the credentials. I know what I'm talking about."

Well, there you have it. It's official. She is right and I am wrong.

Happy Day for People Who are Mothers.

May 13, 2012

A Good Month for Awareness

Last week somebody urged me to write a story about Parkinson's disease because April is Parkinson's Awareness Month.

You betcha. I'll get right on that. And then I'll write a story about autism, because April also is Autism Awareness Month.

April is Oral Cancer Awareness Month, too.

And STD Awareness Month.

And Sexual Assault Awareness Month.

And Distracted Driver Awareness Month.

And Child Abuse Prevention Month.

And Disaster Preparedness Month.

And Stress Awareness Month.

On a less stressful note, April also is National Poetry Month and Jazz Appreciation Month and National Garden Month and National Landscape Architecture Month.

In some circles, it's Water Conservation Month or Occupational Therapy Month or Mathematics Awareness Month or Financial Literacy Month.

If demographics are your thing, April can be Asian Heritage Month and National Arab American Heritage Month and National Minority Health Month.

Let the record show we also are moving through National Greyhound Adoption Month (presumably the dogs, not the buses).

It's National Volunteer Month, too, but how could a person possibly decide?

News releases about these things often are delivered by publicists who apparently jump out of bed each morning like kangaroos in heat. The National Patient Organization for Primary Immunodeficiency Diseases declares, "April is Primary Immunodeficiency Awareness Month!" Yes, with an exclamation point.

Woo-hoo!

But we're not here to ridicule the ridiculous trend in which every special-interest group in America unilaterally awards itself its own month. We're here to ridicule the month's single most ridiculous PR release.

Because April's burdens also include National Car Care Month, some genius from the Engine Rebuilders Council in Washington put out a "news release" saying April is "the perfect time to consider a rebuilt engine."

Now, why would we want to spend a bunch of money to rebuild the engine in an aging car? Because, he says, "a rebuilt engine gets better gas mileage."

Now *there's* a deal. Let's spend $3,000 to rebuild an engine so we can improve our gas mileage.

Why, if we could jack up our mileage by, say, 3 miles per gallon, we could pay for the job in—oh, about 10 years.

Good thing April is National Humor Month.

April 10, 2012

Sensitivity Runs Amok in Federal League

In the overall scheme of things, the handmade signs on the wall of Hoover High School's gymnasium seemed rather bland.

But apparently some people aren't looking at the overall scheme of things.

The North Canton Hoover volleyball team was hosting the Jackson Polar Bears. In keeping with a time-honored tradition across the land, a handful of school-spirited students had painted signs encouraging the home team to vanquish the visitors.

As usual, the kids were big on alliteration. Among the signs: "Bury the Bears."

Now, even PETA would recognize that the Hoover students were not, in fact, urging their classmates to take the lives of the visiting players and bury their carcasses in shallow graves in the end zone of Hoover's football field. But the following morning, Jackson's athletic director phoned Hoover's athletic director and politely complained.

Honest.

Now, if the Hoover kids had written, "Chop Off the Polar Bears' Heads and Kick Them Around the Gym Floor Until Their Eyeballs Fall Out," one might be able to work up a bit of outrage.

And that's probably closer to what the Federal League had in mind a few years ago when it enacted a rule that signs cannot denigrate a visiting team.

But wait. This gets better.

Ten days after Jackson woofed about Hoover's signs, Jackson's official publicist sent out an electronic mailing to "Friends of Jackson Local Schools" requesting that everyone save a number of upcoming dates for various Jackson events. The first one: "Burn the Bulldog."

"A bonfire and school-spirit rally for the whole community. Thursday, Sept. 24, 7:30 p.m. Fife Stadium."

Ahem.

The Bulldog, in this case, is the Canton McKinley football team (not to be confused with the Bulldogs from Stow).

So one wonders: Why can we burn a bulldog but not bury a bear? Because bulldogs are more plentiful? Because they're uglier? Do bears simply have better lobbyists?

Federal League Commissioner Joe Eaton says that, in the name of good sportsmanship, league rules prohibit any dig at an opponent.

Now, good sportsmanship is a wonderful goal. But really—"Bury the Bears" is offensive?

According to Eaton, you couldn't even paint a sign that reads, "Take the Bear for a Walk."

"You cannot have any signs other than positive signs for your school, like 'Go Bears,' " he says. "That's fine."

In other words, kids, you shall nevermore "Pound the Perry Panthers."

For the record, Hoover's was hardly the most egregious violation. A few years ago, Canton McKinley students posted a sign that read: "Murda Hoova."

Not good. For one thing, it lacked alliteration. Shoulda waited till they played Manchesta.

Sept. 24, 2009

Coventry Township Man Didn't Fight for This

It's hard to pinpoint Alex Radisa's first thought when he was randomly detained and interrogated by people wearing uniforms and guns.

Was he thinking about his grandparents, who risked everything to leave their Croatian homeland and come to the United States in search of freedom?

Was he thinking about his father, who died while fighting against the totalitarian Axis powers during World War II?

Was he thinking about the 11 months he served in Vietnam after enlisting in the U.S. Navy in an attempt to stop the rise of communist repression?

Radisa eventually flashed on all of those things after being pulled over by Summit County sheriff's deputies at South Main Street and Killian Road last September.

Law enforcement officials refer to the drill as a "sobriety checkpoint" designed to catch drunken drivers. They plan to set up another one tomorrow night near Blossom Music Center.

But Radisa doesn't drink. So he refers to the practice as an "illegal search." He claims sobriety checkpoints are a clear violation of the U.S. Constitution.

And if you don't think Alex Radisa is absolutely correct, you just haven't thought about it enough.

That includes the U.S. Supreme Court, which has inexplicably upheld the practice.

"They were searching me for alcohol—either in my car or in my body. There was no alcohol. They had no reason to pull me over. I didn't do anything."

Some of you are no doubt muttering that Radisa would change his tune if someone he loved were injured by a drunken driver.

Well, guess what? Radisa's sister was crippled by a drunken driver 4½ years ago. Radisa takes care of her in his modest brick ranch in Coventry Township.

So this guy knows—firsthand—the horrors a drunken driver can inflict. He would dearly love to get every one of them off the road.

But he also knows—firsthand—the horrors of a police state.

When he served with the Mobile Riverine Force in Vietnam, "the South Vietnamese had no rights whatsoever. We could stop and search them, check their ID cards. If we didn't like them, we could detain them. We also carried blacklists. . . . I've seen this with my own eyes."

The night he was stopped, Radisa wasn't in any particular hurry, and he estimates the entire incident took only 10 minutes.

He was returning home at 10:30 from the Croatian Club. He loves to go there to watch the old folks do Kolo dances. It reminds him of his childhood.

But he was stunned when he was pulled over and questioned while a videotape camera rolled and members of Mothers Against Drunk Driving gawked.

"What the police did was illegal. This is plainly stated in the Constitution. It's not ambiguous. Anybody with an eighth-grade education can read this and understand that they have to have probable cause to stop you."

When asked whether the ends justify the means, he replies, "That's the very same thing Josef Stalin said."

Bingo.

If people in uniforms can sniff around inside your car, eventually they'll be knocking on your front door.

Don't mind us, folks. We just need to poke around in your closets for a few minutes. Sorry to inconvenience you, but—as you know—illegal drugs are a serious problem. And so is pornography. And so is. . . .

Radisa, 52, a straightforward fellow with dark red hair and a beard, is not a candidate to join a militia group. He deeply distrusts the militias, saying many of the leaders harbor a hidden agenda involving white supremacy. But he understands the pull.

"I love my country," he says, a bit of moisture pooling in his large brown eyes. "[But] they are slowly but surely taking our constitutional rights away from us."

Alex Radisa risked his life for those rights.

When the replica of the Vietnam Veterans Memorial came to Akron earlier this month, Radisa was part of the honor guard. Stood watch from 4 to 8 a.m. In the dark. In the rain. Loved every minute. Considered it a privilege.

"There are 51 names on that wall from my task force alone," Radisa says. "I would hate to think these men died so their own country would turn into a police state."

June 23, 1997

Lane Hogs Should Get Tickets

Well, here's some legislation we can all get behind. That's because we've all been behind one.

A Left Lane Hog, that is.

You know the scenario. Two lanes of asphalt stretching out in the same direction. In the right lane are vehicles traveling at or below the speed limit. Faster vehicles are in the left lane—except for Mr. or Ms. Left-Lane Hog.

Mr./Ms. LLH is tooling along at 6 mph below the speed limit—totally oblivious to the 37 cars locked in behind him/her, piloted by 37 motorists who are absolutely seething.

Are these LLHs so ignorant that they don't even know they're not supposed to be in the left lane?

Are they so oblivious to their surroundings that they can't see that 37 motorists are trapped behind then, trying to contain 37 cases of road rage?

Worse, are they self-appointed keepers of what they unilaterally deem to be the proper speed limit?

Worst yet, are they in a bad mood and trying to ruin the day for everybody else, just out of spite?

Ignorant . . . oblivious . . . self-centered . . . nasty. It doesn't much matter when we're running 10 minutes late to pick up our kids or trying to get to the bank before it closes. Left Lane Hogs are a menace to society. And it's time to rub them out.

Six states have legislation on their books to do just that. In Kentucky, Maine, Massachusetts, New Jersey, Pennsylvania and Washington, you are permitted to use the left lane only for passing or turning left. Otherwise, you will get a ticket.

Six other states require you to move right if you are blocking traffic in the left lane.

Most of the rest of the states follow the Uniform Vehicle Code, the appropriate section of which reads:

"Upon all roadways, any vehicle proceeding at less than the normal speed of traffic at the time and place and under the conditions then existing shall be driven in the right-hand lane then available for traffic."

Please note that the operative word is not the "legal" speed of traffic. It is the "normal" speed of traffic. If you're driving 60 mph in a 55 mph zone and everybody else is going 65, you are legally obligated to move your butt over.

Only Alaska permits drivers to stay left if they are going the precise speed limit. The trend is overwhelmingly in the other direction. In fact, right now, Illinois is enacting legislation that would kick everyone out of the left lane unless they are passing. It sailed through the Illinois House, 99 to 13.

The states that have the legislation are enforcing it. Soon after a bill passed in the state of Washington, police stopped 9,591 drivers for "impeding traffic" in one year in just one congressional district.

Before you start ranting about lunatics taking over the highways, please note that the creator of the Illinois bill is a former police chief. His name is John Millner, and he wants LLHs to be ticketed. Millner says his bill is a much-needed antidote to the road-rage epidemic.

Are we caving in to rage? Hardly. In my experience, most cases of road rage are highly justified. We're just trying to find ways to get the attention of the ignoramuses and keep them from triggering violent reactions in normal folks.

In a recent article on Edmunds.com, an excellent automotive website, a writer made a solid, practical suggestion:

"Here's a simple rule for anyone entering the passing lane: If it takes you more than 20 seconds to get past a 'slower' moving vehicle, you are going too slow yourself to justify use of the left lane. Remain in the right lane, even if it means following the same vehicle for another 100 miles.

"If you think this rule sounds like a harsh edict meant to keep certain drivers and vehicle types from ever entering the fast lane— good, you're starting to get the idea."

June 6, 2003

Copley Case is Not About Race

Here we go again.

Even in the year 2011—148 years after the Emancipation Procla-
mation . . . 48 years after MLK moved the nation with his "Dream"
speech . . . three years after this country elected a president of color
largely because 42 million white people voted for him—a significant percentage of the population seems incapable of believing that
racial motives aren't involved in every human interaction.

The latest nonracial issue to be thrown into the racial category is
the controversial court case in which an African-American woman
was convicted of a felony for falsifying documents to enable her kids
to attend a better school and get free lunches.

At this point, "School Mom" is in danger of surpassing "Octomom"
in cumulative publicity, and I hesitate to add yet another pile of
words to this saga. But I decline to stand idly by while false accusations are flying.

One emailer wrote to me: "This crime didn't require a jail sentence, and I absolutely 100 percent think that if [the judge] had
been looking at a white woman with the exact same hardworking
background and statistics, there wouldn't have been . . . .

"Secondly, this never, ever would have been [tried as a] felony
had she been white with an identical background. It would have
been a plea-bargained misdemeanor."

Wrote another, following my column that asserted the verdict
was correct: "You certainly have the support of all the racists in
town. Is that who you want to be associated with?

"You will say that you are not a racist yourself, and that racism is
not a prerequisite for agreeing with your position. However, as the
saying goes, if you lie down with dogs, you get fleas."

Even the woman's attorney, Kerry O'Brien, couldn't resist tossing
the race card into the middle of his failed motion to dismiss the
charges: "The fact that the defendants are African-American also
raises the specter of improper racial segregation and prosecution
with respect to this case," he wrote.

What a crock.

Here are some facts.

From 2005 through Friday afternoon, the Copley-Fairlawn School District formally confronted 48 families whose children were illegally attending its schools. The breakdown:

- 29 families were black.
- 15 families were white.
- two families were Asian.
- one family was Pacific Islander.
- one family was multiracial.

Question: If Copley went after Kelley Williams-Bolar because she is black, why didn't Copley take the 28 other black families to court?

Answer: Because those families didn't do what Williams-Bolar did. Those families paid what they owed and immediately withdrew from the school or made arrangements so their children were legally residing in the district.

Williams-Bolar was not singled out because of her skin color. She was singled out because—unlike 47 other families of varying colors—she openly and continually defied the school system, insisting that her kids lived in the district when they were living with her in Akron, and lying about her income and child support so her kids would get free lunches.

That's what a jury decided unanimously—a jury that included four blacks.

Moreover, when Williams-Bolar cried racism two years ago, the U.S. Department of Education's Office of Civil Rights investigated her situation and concluded that race had nothing to do with it.

The office issued a four-page ruling on Dec. 10, 2008, that proclaimed white and black families in the same situation had been treated the same.

As if the local hubbub were not enough, the story has gone national, and the nation is getting a staggering amount of misinformation.

A writer whose column was posted on the high-traffic website Salon opined: "We can't possibly ignore the racial aspect of this situation. A poor BLACK woman on public assistance is being jailed for sending her kids to the rich white school."

If the writer had bothered to check, he would have discovered that this "rich white school" has a student body that is 17 percent BLACK—along with 4 percent Asian and 3 percent multiracial.

That's called diversity. And that's one reason Copley-Fairlawn is a great school system.

Look: I realize skin color consistently colors our perception of the world and the world's perception of us. I also am fully aware that racism is still alive and well in the hearts of millions of Americans—white and black.

But attributing nonracial motives to racism only drives another wedge between people who don't need any more wedges between them.

Jan. 30, 2011

Some Advice For Al Sharpton

Dear Al:

I didn't attend your dog and pony show on Thursday night at the Mountain of the Lord Fellowship Church in Akron because I have long viewed you not as a man of the cloth but as a charlatan, much like our own Ernest Angley.

Both of you cloak yourselves in virtue, but both of you are, at your core, frauds.

Angley claims he can cure AIDS by slapping people on the forehead. You claim to be solving society's ills by dealing out the race card—day after day after day after day.

I have no idea why the media continue to treat you with such reverence. You have somehow become the default arbiter on the topic of discrimination, the go-to guy for every person with a notebook or camera.

I would have thought you would have lost your credibility after slandering half of New York's law-enforcement community while rushing to the defense of monumental liar Tawana Brawley.

So I promised myself I would not write a word about your visit, because even when people write bad things, that only adds lumens to your spotlight. But I am simply incapable of allowing your latest absurd pronouncements to pass without comment.

With lights blazing and cameras whirring, you declared: "I think this woman should be saluted, not arrested."

Perhaps a statue would be in order. Maybe we should put Kelley Williams-Bolar right next to Charles Goodyear at the Ocasek building, or adjacent to Col. Simon Perkins on the University of Akron campus.

As if that comment weren't dumb enough, you added this: "Too many of us adjust, rather than having society adjust to us."

Well, Al, you may want to give that concept a little more thought.

Maybe you can find a moment or two to get away from the photographers and videographers, go off by yourself to a quiet place, sit down and reflect. Maybe you could even pray on it.

Picture the kind of world we would have if society adjusted to School Mom, rather than the other way around.

In review:

She lied about her income.

She lied about her child support.

She lied about her place of residence.

She lied about serving in the military.

She lied about lying.

She taught her children that lying is fine if it enables you to get what you want.

And she thinks none of this should disqualify her from being a schoolteacher.

Williams-Bolar also claimed she was a victim of age discrimination because she was 40.

Forty! Omar Vizquel is 43 and playing major league baseball!

And, of course, she claimed she was prosecuted because she is black.

Al, let's take a closer look at her lie about serving her country.

She admitted during her trial that when she received an envelope in 2008 from the Copley-Fairlawn School system, she returned it unopened, writing, "Deployed overseas for eight months."

According to the official court transcript, this exchange took place immediately after that admission:

PROSECUTOR: "Are you in the military?"

WILLIAMS-BOLAR: "No."

PROSECUTOR: "Have you ever been in the military?"

WILLIAMS-BOLAR: "Never."

PROSECUTOR: "Have you ever been deployed?"

WILLIAMS-BOLAR: "No. But I have been harassed."

Well, that's pretty much the same thing, isn't it?

While many of her fellow Akron residents were being shipped away from home into the ongoing nightmare of Iraq and Afghanistan—some of them losing limbs and lives—School Mom felt totally justified in using those people as fodder for her lie machine.

And when she was called to task on it, she reacted with indignation.

I will grant you this, Al: You did make some excellent points about education. In many parts of this country, the educational system is a mess.

But using School Mom to make that point is like rushing to the defense of Bernie Madoff to criticize the excesses of Wall Street. It just doesn't compute.

But then again, you never let logic block the view of the cameras, do you?

Bob

Feb. 20, 2011

Governor Tanks Case for School Mom

Unbelievable.

I knew the governor's approval rating was in the dumper, but I honestly never believed he would stoop to this level.

Of course, when the first 20 people a politician appoints to his Cabinet are white, and 16 are men, and the biggest newspaper in the state runs their photos across the top of the front page like prison mug shots, that politician has a lot of ground to make up among other demographic groups.

You've probably heard by now that our fearless leader has decided that poor, misunderstood Kelley Williams-Bolar has suffered enough. He reduced her ongoing felonious falsifications to misdemeanors.

"School Mom," as she has become internationally known, was abused by the evil judicial system, so Ohio's highest-ranking official stepped in to dispense justice. Yessir.

Did John Kasich even *read* the report by the Ohio Parole Board?

He was the guy who assigned those eight people the task of analyzing the case! And those folks—whose jobs consist of making precisely these types of character judgments—held a huge hearing in Columbus at which all parties were given plenty of time to talk. Testimony went on for six hours.

The board listened and asked questions. And then it assembled a 16-page report that said, in essence: Kelley Williams-Bolar deserves clemency when hell freezes over.

Board members took 44 days to analyze the testimony. Kasich took a Labor Day weekend to blow them off.

Kasich's approach was the equivalent of an NFL referee watching a replay challenge with his eyes closed. Nothing was going to sway him from his previous notion.

He said as much in Wednesday's short news release: "When I first heard about this situation, it seemed to me that the penalty was excessive for the offense."

If nothing was going to sway him from his first impression—

including the facts—why go through the charade of asking for outside assistance?

The board's report was not exactly ambiguous.

"Williams-Bolar was faced with a no more difficult situation than any other working parent who must ensure that their children are safe during, before and after school. . . . Most parents find legitimate and legal options to address this issue. Ms. Williams-Bolar's only response was to be deceitful."

The board also said the prosecution was not selective, the jury "correctly applied" laws that are "appropriately crafted . . . to protect public institutions from being intentionally defrauded" and that the judge "responded with appropriate sentencing, given the defendant's wholesale refusal to accept any responsibility for her actions.

"Any effort to [reduce the sentence] . . . would communicate exactly the wrong message."

Mind you, the board does not consist of a bunch of Nazis. Its chairwoman, Cynthia Mausser, once worked as an assistant state public defender, fighting for inmates at parole-revocation hearings.

By reducing the charges, Kasich not only blew off all eight members of the parole board, but also all 12 members of the Summit County jury who decided Williams-Bolar's actions were worthy of felony convictions.

The main thing that is consistently lost in all of this is that, to reach a plea bargain, both sides have to be willing to bargain. Williams-Bolar adamantly maintained her innocence throughout the entire judicial process (and well beyond). Should everyone whose legal strategy doesn't pan out get another shot?

Maybe Kasich didn't make his judgment with one eye on the most recent Quinnipiac poll—which shows him with a stunningly low 35 percent approval rating—and another eye on the 184,000 pro-Williams-Bolar emails his office received from Change.org and the 70,000 names on a petition from ColorOfChange.org. But given the circumstances, nothing else comes to mind.

I wonder how Kasich would like it if Williams-Bolar were teaching his own kids?

Oops, no chance of that. As the board put it, she "is nowhere near to obtaining a college degree in any discipline, let alone in education or early childhood development."

In other words, all that gnashing of teeth about School Mom losing her impending teaching career was a farce.

Bottom line: The governor of this state says you can rip off a public school system for $30,000 in tuition (which Copley-Fairlawn will never get back), lie about your residency, your income, your child support, your military service, your insurance coverage, your eligibility for home heating assistance and subsidized lunches . . . essentially lie ad infinitum, and the only thing you're risking is a slap on the wrist.

Nice lesson we're teaching our kids.

Perhaps it will be part of the curriculum at Kasich's charter schools.

Sept. 11, 2011

Wadsworth Man Hammered Only By Association

Jerry Seabrook is a statistic.

Or, rather, he used to be.

On June 23, he was a drunken driver. On Aug. 9, he wasn't.

Trouble is, nobody bothered to change the numbers.

But let's take this from the top.

It's a beautiful Saturday afternoon, early summer, in a cozy middle-class neighborhood in Wadsworth.

Life is good. Seabrook is 70 years old now, retired and plays a lot of golf. When he's not on the links, he and his wife are probably at the local public library, delivering Meals on Wheels or immersed in a project at Grace Lutheran Church.

The guy has paid his dues. He grew up poor in the Dover area, worked his way through college, served in the Army, taught school for six years and then spent the bulk of his working life, 32 years, as a pension analyst at Bridgestone-Firestone.

Now that the kids are gone, the Seabrooks do a lot of socializing. So late that June afternoon, they hop into his 2002 Ford Escape and head to the home of longtime friends in the former Northampton Township area of Cuyahoga Falls.

Another couple has been invited, too, and the six of them begin a pleasant get-together.

The initial topic is the news about Jesse Marie Davis, whose body has just been found not far from the house. Seabrook mentions seeing a slew of police cars on Bath Road.

When the host offers cocktails, Seabrook asks for a Manhattan. His wife, Shirley, usually has one glass of wine before switching to coffee, but on this day she is taking a prescription medication and doesn't want to mix it with alcohol.

The group gathers around the television to watch the 6 o'clock news. When the newscast is over, they head out to the patio to chat. About 20 minutes later, Seabrook finishes his drink.

The host pours him another. Before Seabrook can finish that one, the guests are summoned to the screened-in porch for dinner. He finishes his second drink while feasting on eggplant Parmesan.

After dinner, it's back to the TV to watch the Cleveland Indians. The Tribe is losing until the ninth, when Victor Martinez hits a dramatic three-run homer.

In the afterglow of that happy ending, the Seabrooks thank their hosts and head home.

Roughly halfway back to Wadsworth, as they're driving south on state Route 21 in Copley Township, they come over a rise and encounter a "sobriety checkpoint." The area is lit up like a high-school football field.

Seabrook isn't the least bit worried. He finished his second drink a little after 7 p.m., and now it's nearly 11. He's a big fellow, too—244 pounds.

So even though a Manhattan is a strong drink (whiskey and vermouth), he knows he is far below the legal limit.

"I've always tried to be a law-abiding citizen," Seabrooks says. "When [the officer] said, 'Have you had any alcohol to drink today?' I said, 'Yeah, I had two Manhattans before dinner.'

"And immediately a flashlight goes into my eyes. He takes a pen and says, 'Keep your head still and follow this.'

"Then he says, 'Pull down there.'

"We sit there for a while, and he asks me to get out. He said, 'I'd like you to take nine steps forward, heel-to-toe, pivot, and walk nine steps back.' So I counted, pivoted and came back.

"We stood there a little while longer and he said, 'Do you think you can count from 42, fifteen digits back?' I said, 'Yeah, I can count farther than that.' I started in—no problem."

But the officer, James Dawson of the Barberton Police Department, one of 20 Summit County law-enforcement agencies that participate in the Summit County OVI Task Force, doesn't think Seabrook's movements are rock solid. He takes the man's driver's license and directs him to a trailer, where he is asked to take a Breathalyzer test.

Seabrook gladly complies, and blows a 0.049—way below the legal limit of 0.08.

"I guess I'm OK to go," he says.

Dawson, who is making $38 an hour in voluntary overtime pay, disagrees. He tells Seabrook to sit tight while he writes a ticket for OVI—Operating a Vehicle under the Influence of alcohol.

On the citation, he plugs in the code 4511.19 A1A and tells Seabrook that if he is found guilty in court he could lose his license for six months and be sent to a rehab school.

Seabrook is dumbfounded.

Dawson hands back the license and instructs Shirley Seabrook to drive home.

The next day, the "drunken driver" drops in on a neighbor who is a lifelong friend and a judge. He shows the Breathalyzer printout and the citation, upon which Dawson has written: "Odor of alcoholic beverage. Admits to drinking. Glassy eyes."

The friend recommends hiring an attorney. So Seabrook hooks up with David Jack of Wadsworth.

The next day, Seabrook picks up his Akron Beacon Journal and reads about himself.

He's not in there by name, but as one of five people arrested for "operating a motor vehicle under the influence of alcohol." His court date is two days away, but his lawyer gets a continuance. And Seabrook continues to stew.

Finally, on the day of the pretrial hearing, the Seabrooks meet the lawyer outside the courtroom. Jack and the prosecutor go into the judge's chambers and emerge less than 15 minutes later. Jack tells Seabrook: "You're free to go. It's been dismissed."

In other words, Seabrook was not driving under the influence of alcohol. But now he's out $750 in legal fees with no recourse for reimbursement.

The checkpoint also ruined what would have been a pleasant Saturday evening. Not only was he detained for an hour (records show he was stopped at 10:54 p.m. and the breath test was given at 11:46), but he spent the next 47 days worrying about losing his license.

If you ask me, the cop who charged Seabrook with drunken driving should be docked $750.

Naturally, his boss disagrees.

Barberton Police Chief Michael Kallai admits that Seabrook was the victim of "an unfortunate set of circumstances," but defends the checkpoints.

(Kallai said the officer did not want to be interviewed.)

"The gentlemen who are out there, the OVI Task Force, are doing their job," Kallai says. "They're stopping traffic, they're checking people and, based on their investigation at that time, this warranted them citing him for driving while intoxicated."

Just doing his job.

Problem is, as Seabrook's lawyer notes, this is not the way America is supposed to work.

"I don't like the whole idea of the OVI checkpoint," Jack says. "I understand the legal rationalization, why the [U.S.] Supreme Court would uphold that [in a split vote]. But to me it's just a fiction used to check people for DUI. And when they do, oftentimes they're overzealous.

"They could have just put this guy back in his car and let him go. He clearly wasn't drinking. He had no bad driving pattern. He had no really significant negativity or much that would make you think he was intoxicated. He just had the odor of alcohol on his breath."

Obviously, the prosecutor had issues with the arrest, too.

Barberton Prosecutor David Fish says that once an officer makes a decision to request a breath test, the driver is technically under arrest and "the die is cast" because most officers are highly reluctant to release someone even with a low reading.

Before administrating the breath test, the cop must make a judgment call. In a normal OVI stop, his judgment is based on a number of factors: bad driving, an odor of alcohol, the eye test and the field test. But at a sobriety checkpoint, the officer is robbed of his first, most important clue: bad driving. That means he has less to go by when trying to assess someone's condition.

"[Dawson] is a very dependable, very competent officer," Fish says. "He made a difficult decision out at the scene. . . . He just didn't feel comfortable placing this guy back on the road."

Fish's decision was much easier.

"When we took a look at the case and saw it was a sobriety checkpoint—that didn't really change our view, but there were things that weren't available to us. There was no evidence of bad driving. We don't have a guy who is staggering. . . .

"A prosecutor's job is to do justice. Justice demanded we dismiss the charges."

The director of the Summit County OVI Task Force isn't fazed.

When it comes to checkpoints, "I don't have any mixed emotions," says Jeff Buck, whose main job is serving as police chief of Reminderville, a burg wedged between Twinsburg, Aurora and Solon.

"I think that we're doing the residents of Summit County and everyone just an enormous amount of good."

Sitting in his tiny office, he fixes you with a steady gaze and says, "I think we're getting people off the road that are killing people when they're drunk, that are driving without insurance, that are driving while they're suspended.

"We're taking people off the roads that have guns, that are carrying concealed weapons, that have felony warrants."

Perhaps the word "sobriety" should be modified.

Summit is one of 10 counties in the state getting roughly $150,000 a year to run these roadblocks. The counties are selected by looking at the statistics for fatal alcohol-related crashes. (Not that those stats are flawless: If you are legally drunk and stopped at a red light, and a sober driver crashes into you from behind, that is classified as an "alcohol-related" crash.)

The money comes from the federal government and is handed out in the form of state grants. But the program is not federally mandated. In fact, 11 states won't have anything to do with it.

Summit's OVI director trots out the battle cry of those who would trample your Fourth Amendment rights: "Driving is a privilege, not a right."

Wrong. Seabrook's taxes helped pay for Route 21. He has every right to drive on it unmolested if he's not breaking any laws.

These roadblocks aren't even catching many drunks.

That night in Copley, the task force questioned 2,422 drivers and found only five—er, make that four—drunks (assuming the two whose cases have not yet been resolved are guilty).

Among the five charged, the highest blood-alcohol content was a hefty 0.176. The next highest was 0.145 which, as recently as 1982, was below the legal limit.

The task force's lousy drunk-catching percentage on June 23 is the norm. In a 2005 case in the Pennsylvania Supreme Court, dissenting justice Russell Nigro cited stats showing that roving patrols are nearly 11 times more effective than checkpoints at catching drunks.

His colleague, Justice Max Baer, noted another problem: "The statistics, while clearly proving the relative ineffectiveness of suspicionless checkpoints, do not in any way account for the substantial intrusion that those checkpoints impose on the lives of law-abiding motorists, who often wait in the backlog of traffic caused by the checkpoints even before enduring the actual stop by police once they reach the checkpoint."

No kidding. You can't stop every car on a highway like state Route 21 without creating a significant traffic jam.

Proponents of the roadblocks are fond of saying the whole stop takes less than a minute. OVI director Buck says he's averaging 28 seconds per car. But nobody ever calculates the amount of time you have to wait in line to get to the checkpoint itself.

Buck admits traffic jams can be an issue. He says he periodically does "a flush" to clear out long lines.

The OVI boss also insists stats don't tell the whole story. "Voluntary compliance through risk of apprehension" is his term for scaring people into not drinking and driving.

Well, he sure got Jerry Seabrook's attention.

In fact, the biggest damage to Seabrook was not to his wallet. The biggest damage came to his perception of his country, the country he served, the country in which he thought he could move about freely.

A search of the Summit County Criminal Justice Information System reveals that Jerald Seabrook did have one prior brush with the law: a speeding ticket in 1997.

(Actually, another listing pops up, too: a "DUI" issued in June. You have to click on the case number to learn that that charge was dismissed. He wanted to have it expunged until he found out that would cost him another $50.)

"I'd just hate to see somebody else get put into the predicament I'm in," he says. "But that's what's going to happen, I'm afraid."

Jerry Seabrook is the face of Middle America. He belongs in a Norman Rockwell painting, sitting on the front porch, waving to the neighbor kid riding by on his bicycle.

If we are indiscriminately stopping, detaining and charging people like Jerry Seabrook, we have taken a wrong turn on our journey to sober streets.

Sept. 26, 2007

DUI Campaign is All for Show

It's just not working.

The people who claim to know what's best for us have tightened the screws harder and harder on social drinkers, saying that will make our highways safer.

But as the total number of traffic fatalities in Ohio continues to drop each year, the number of alcohol-related fatalities continues to rise.

The state lowered the blood-alcohol limit in July 2003. And from 2002 through 2006, alcohol-related fatalities *increased* 3 percent.

By contrast, total traffic deaths during that same period declined by a whopping 15 percent.

Why is one going up and the other going down?

Overall highway safety is improving because our cars are safer (more air bags, for example), our roads are safer (such as shock-absorbing guardrails) and more people are wearing seat belts.

Alcohol-related deaths are on the rise because state and national legislators—influenced by well-financed, media-savvy pressure groups such as MADD—have been making all the wrong moves.

Ohio's definition of "drunken driving" has grown ever more inclusive. The preferred terminology has gone from "DWI" (driving while intoxicated) to "DUI" (driving under the influence) to "OVI" (operating a vehicle while impaired).

The state also has fallen in love with sobriety checkpoints. In just two years, the number of drivers halted annually by county OVI Task Forces has more than doubled, to nearly 118,000.

During those stops, police have a harder time determining who might be a menace because they haven't witnessed any erratic driving. So they're more likely to charge someone who isn't a problem.

In short, we have very nearly criminalized social drinking without reducing the highway carnage one iota.

The increase in alcohol-related deaths is not a function of more drivers on the road. We can confirm that with a quick look at the number of annual deaths per every 100,000 drivers.

Those numbers are even more dramatic: In the last six years, alcohol-related fatalities per 100,000 Ohio motorists surged 31 percent—even though the total death rate per 100,000 dropped 11 percent.

So what are we doing wrong? Glad you asked.

The problem is not responsible social drinkers. The problem is guys like Jess R. Brown of Barberton, who qualified for his 20th drunken-driving conviction last year while out on bond for what turned into his 19th conviction.

Brown didn't get caught at checkpoints; he got caught because he kept smashing into things and hurting people. His last conviction came after he plowed into a Norton woman head-on.

Do you think this guy cut back his consumption when the blood-alcohol limit was lowered 0.02 percentage points? Do you think this guy would be deterred by the possibility of encountering a sobriety checkpoint?

Or how about Todd Manley of Hudson, proud owner of 18 convictions? One of his most recent ones came after he rammed into a parked car in Stow and hurt a teenage girl.

Randy L. McFadden of Mogadore is another member of the double-digit club, having earned his 10th conviction a year ago after he was caught speeding.

Although these guys are the stars, they are by no means unique. Through the end of last year, more than 33,000 Ohio residents had five or more drunken-driving convictions.

In other words, we could fill more than three-quarters of Jacobs Field with Ohioans who have five or more convictions.

Five or more!

We simply haven't figured out a way to keep repeat offenders off the road. Taking away their driver's license doesn't work, because they just drive without one. Throwing them in jail even for long periods of time doesn't work, either, because they come out just as thirsty as when they went in.

That is the real drunken-driving problem. And that is where we ought to be spending our money.

It's not as if better ideas aren't out there. In fact, we have some spectacularly promising programs. But the funding for those programs is a mere pittance compared with the money we're pouring into sobriety checkpoints.

For the fiscal year 2008, Ohio will dole out $2,475,000 in federal money for OVI Task Forces and related programs and equipment. That is 85 percent of the total budget the Governor's Highway Safety Office is devoting to combat drunken driving.

Only $425,000—less than 15 percent—will be used for a "DUI Court" pilot program that has shown great promise in a several counties, including Summit.

Since the local program began last May, 35 repeat drunken-drivers have been enrolled and not a single one has re-offended. All but two have stopped drinking.

Akron Municipal Judge Alison McCarty began lobbying the state to fund a DUI court after witnessing how well the local "drug court" had functioned for more than a decade. Last year, she got $128,700 to launch one. This year's budget is $148,700.

The program combines a full year of intensive probation supervision with a graduated scale of penalties for those who don't cooperate and rewards for those who do.

It targets the hard-core people with at least two drunken-driving convictions in the previous six years who have blown more than twice the legal limit.

"With two exceptions, they're all staying sober," McCarty says. "They're maintaining employment. They're not driving illegally.

"The couple that have had problems we've put into IBH [Interval Brotherhood Home] because they just couldn't stay out in the community and lick it."

The keys to the program are direct involvement by judges and probation officers, coupled with new technology.

During their first month, offenders appear before a judge every week, then every six weeks after that. They also meet with a caseworker every week for a year.

In addition, they must submit to one or more monitoring programs.

All participants begin by wearing a "SCRAM" cuff. (That's the acronym for a brand name, Secure, Continuous, Remote Alcohol-Monitoring.) It is worn around the ankle, and if an offender drinks any alcohol, the cuff detects it in the skin and sends the information to a modem, which phones in the bad report.

Some offenders are required to place a MEMS unit in their home. That's another brand-name acronym for a machine that is essentially a Breathalyzer with a camera.

It is programmed to randomly signal the offender to take a test two or three times a day. As the person is blowing, a digital photo is taken, transmitted by phone and compared with the photo on file.

Offenders pay $30 to $360 a month, based on their income.

These relatively new gizmos have made DUI courts feasible because, unlike drugs, which stay in the body for days, alcohol passes through in a matter of hours, enabling users to dodge detection more easily.

"We have not had one person test positive for alcohol while on the SCRAMS," McCarty says. "They take it seriously, and it really helps. It gives them the start they need in sobriety. Some of these people haven't been sober for more than a day or two at a time for months or years.

"I'm really optimistic."

McCarty says Summit is only the third county in the state to try the program, and the only large urban county.

Technology also is the key to keeping people off the road who just can't kick the habit. But Ohio lawmakers and courts are lagging behind on that issue, too.

At least 23 other states require ignition interlocks on the vehicles of repeat offenders. Those units also are similar to the Breathalyzer: the driver must blow into a tube; if alcohol is detected, the car won't start.

New Mexico is in the forefront. In that state, interlocks are mandatory even for first offenders. From the start of 2005, when the law was changed, through the end of last year, New Mexico's drunken-driving deaths fell 13 percent.

One problem with the standard breath interlock is that someone else can blow into the tube.

Some devices try to combat that by including "rolling retests," in which a driver is required to blow again while the vehicle is moving. That doesn't preclude someone else from blowing, either, but the other person would have to come along. And if the other person is sober, he or she might as well drive.

The national average rental, paid by the offender, is $60 a month.

An even better solution: an invention called The DUI Gauntlet.

A local woman has been pushing that device since 2004 to excellent reviews. But sales haven't come close to matching the reviews.

Elaine Futrell of Akron developed the system based on the premise that drunks aren't known for their lightning-quick reflexes.

After putting the key in the ignition, the driver has only seconds to perform a series of tasks—for instance, turning on and off the left-turn signal, pushing the brake pedal, turning on and off the parking lights, turning on and off the right-turn signal.

If you can't complete the list within the allotted time in three tries, the car won't start for four hours.

You can't switch drivers easily because the engine stops when you move off the seat. And, because the system takes a while to master, and the computer demands continuous improvement as the driver grows accustomed to it, a sober newcomer would have a tough time making the grade in three tries.

All attempts are recorded for future examination by the probation department.

The biggest drawback is the cost: $150 to install, $60 to $95 per month rental and another $150 to uninstall.

But Futrell's machine, unlike the breath detectors, has the added advantage of stopping people who are high on drugs.

Futrell has made a couple of modest inroads in other parts of the country, but she has had trouble getting the ear of Ohio legislators.

Apparently, they can't kick their sobriety-checkpoint habit.

Perhaps they're addicted to the thrill: Television news crews trotting out to the scene, shooting the bright lights and surprised faces, then slapping that footage on the air, where it looks for all the world as if we're fixing the drunken-driving problem.

We're not.

Dec. 26, 2007

Anonymous Posters Need a Backbone

If Ohio.com, the Beacon Journal's Internet site, offered message boards on the morning of Sept. 11, 2001, here's what would have shown up:

- "Borrrrring! Another non-story by the Leaking Urinal. Why don't you guys find some real news?"
- "I know somebody who works for the city, and he says Don Plusquellic is behind this."
- "I read this yesterday in the Plain Dealer."
- "I know a person who knows a person whose brother-in-law was told first-hand by an Akron policeman, or maybe it was a sheriff's deputy, that the mayor of New York City was seen by a neighbor hanging upside down in a tree, naked, next to a chimpanzee, eating a banana and drinking shots of vodka just minutes before the second plane hit the tower."
- "You guys write a whole story about a big attack and don't even tell us who did it? The usual third-rate reporting by a dying newspaper."
- "Your liberal rag is playing this up to make George Bush look bad. Did you really have to devote all that space to one incident?"
- "Nobody is going to find the real truth here. The traditional media are in Bush's pocket. Google 'George Bush' and 'Twin Towers' and you'll see that Bush ordered the attack. It's a known fact."
- "I knew we shouldn't have drafted Tim Couch."
- "You're a moron. It isn't Couch's fault. It's that stupid coach of his. He doesn't have a clue. I knew it the instant they hired him."
- "I feel sorry for the victims' families."
- "I don't feel sorry for anybody. All those people in the Twin Towers were crooked businessmen. I bought some stock from a brokerage firm that had offices there and it lost money. You reap what you sew."
- "Tim Couch doesn't have an offensive line. If you don't get enough time, even Bernie Kosar would be lousy."
- "I miss Regina Brett."

- "I'll bet Don Robart loved this attack because it shows how easy it would be to knock down State Road Shopping Center."
- "My cousin's friend's brother plays for the Browns, and he says Tim Couch is out every night until dawn snorting coke and shooting smack."
- "The Beacon Journal screws up again. I can tell from the pictures this is Chicago, not New York."
- "Channel 5 had this story last week."
- "This never would have happened if John S. Knight were still alive."

For those of you who don't have access to the Internet, we should probably elaborate.

Employees of the Beacon Journal write stories and columns that not only are printed in the newspaper but posted on our website. At the bottom of almost every story, we invite all comers to comment.

The idea is the same as it is with letters to the editor: To allow readers to express their own opinion, offer additional information, suggest changes or anything else within reason.

Unlike traditional letters to the editor, though, Internet posters don't have to use their real names—and most don't. As a result, the level of discourse is not always what it might be.

In fact, we get a remarkable number of Internet readers who delight in taking anonymous potshots at the people in the stories, the people who write the stories and the organization that distributes the stories. The comments often have little to do with the subject at hand. They often are factually incorrect. And they can be incredibly rude and hurtful.

Example? This was the second comment under a news story about a local man who had drowned just hours earlier, on July 4: "That will surely put a damper on any holiday festivities. Wonder if he had 'the big one' before he hit the water??"

Here's another post on the same story: "I suspect he was drinking and playing grab@#$. That's what happens when people are trying to be funny."

Nice compassion.

Sometimes, the cheap shots get so nasty—and/or libelous—that management removes the whole discussion. That inevitably brings howls of protest from posters who—apparently with a straight face—accuse the Beacon Journal of depriving them of their freedom of speech.

Where in the First Amendment does it say a private business is obligated to give voice to anonymous jerks?

You want freedom of speech? Fine. Buy a printing press. Launch a website. Hand out fliers on the street corner. Say anything you want on your own dime and your own time.

That is freedom of speech.

And if you do say absolutely anything you feel like saying, you may discover that freedom of speech is not absolute. Accuse somebody of criminal activity without proof and you are the one who could wind up in court.

In short, we'd all be better off if, instead of immediately hitting the "send" key after indulging your basest instincts, you would pause for a moment to consider what you're doing.

People who really want to change things for the better, rather than just show off, don't hide behind screen names and twist the facts.

If the Internet had been around in 1775, the fellow who said, "Give me liberty or give me death!" would not have identified himself as "Pato2."

Sept. 22, 2009

The Great Wall of Fairlawn Has Sequel

Four years ago, in an attempt to avoid typecasting, I vowed I would never write another column about one of my pet peeves: sound walls.

But I am simply incapable of letting the latest atrocity pass without a rant.

Besides, I'm not the only one. Akron attorney Christopher Esker is on the same page. He shot me an email soon after he noticed that a 600-foot-long stretch of the Great Wall of Fairlawn had been torn down for no apparent reason.

"Can you get to the bottom of just why [the Ohio Department of Transportation] seems to be disassembling and burying on-site at least a portion of the fairly recently erected faux brick sound wall?"

Esker was referring to activity along the southbound side of Interstate 77 between Cleveland-Massillon Road and the Miller/Ridgewood exit.

I had noticed it, too, and assumed a major problem had cropped up unrelated to the wall, such as the collapse of a storm sewer. After all, nobody would tear down a wall that had been erected at enormous cost—more than $1 million per mile—a mere five years earlier.

This wall is actually the Great Wall of Fairlawn II, not to be confused with the original, a steel-and-wood, $860,000 monstrosity that started to sink three months after being built in 1994.

But the construction of Great Wall III is not the result of an issue unrelated to the wall.

Wait until you hear why you and I are donating another $409,000 for this same stretch of highway.

A nearby homeowner complained to ODOT that the noise was still too loud. So ODOT went out and investigated. And what ODOT discovered, according to a spokesman, was this: "It was determined that the existing noise-wall section does not block the line of sight to all I-77 traffic from the first floors of the existing houses."

The *line of sight?* I thought these things were *sound* walls!

Well, ODOT says, its regulations call for the walls to block the view, too.

Wait, it gets even better.

The reason ODOT didn't comply with its own regulation in the first place is that when the engineering wizards drew up the plan, they mistook the walkout basements for first floors, and mistook the first floors for second floors.

I swear I am not making this up.

So now our tax dollars are being used to yank out a 5-year-old wall, which was 7 feet high, and build a new wall, which will be 9 feet high.

The wall also will be lengthened by 180 feet.

The person who complained lives on a street—White Tail Ridge Drive—on which the three most recent home sales were $303,000, $375,000 and $382,000.

In other words, you and I are paying an enormous amount of money—again—to improve the personal aesthetics of a handful of people living in $350,000 houses.

I'd like to believe that exposing this kind of misuse of public money would have an impact, but I no longer have much faith.

After all, nothing changed after I wrote half a dozen columns during the 1990s quoting national acoustical experts who said sound walls are largely ineffective for any homeowner who doesn't live right next to the wall, and can actually be counterproductive for others—*increasing* the noise for people living as much as a quarter-mile away.

Nothing changed in 2003 after I went down and interviewed a bunch of people who lived right behind a new wall along I-77 just south of Belden Village and discovered they didn't particularly like their new wall or thought it did much good. Their *$7 million* wall.

Nothing changed after I pointed out that the federal requirement for walls to be built whenever a freeway is widened applies only if a community wants the walls, and that the local ODOT district's definition of "the community" has been limited to people living within 400 feet of a proposed wall.

When ODOT asked those people in 2006 about a plan to build $3.6 million worth of walls through Akron, Fairlawn and Copley, 90 percent didn't care enough to respond.

So ODOT asked again, warning that walls would not be built if residents didn't express more interest. The second time, 83 percent still didn't respond. Of the tiny fraction who did, a majority wanted them. And that was good enough for ODOT.

ODOT's sound-wall fetish was bad enough before the economy tanked. Today, with state and local budgets flat-lining, it seems criminal.

July 12, 2011

Super Stupid

Here's something to chew on during your big Super Bowl party today.

A 24-year-old Massillon woman, Taryn Chojnowski, was sentenced to 31 years in prison after Summit County officials charged her with four felonies. Chojnowski's offense? Prostitution. When you cut through all the fancy legalese—stuff like "conspiracy to engage in a pattern of corrupt activity"—she got 31 years for having consensual sex.

Meanwhile, one of the teams in today's big game, the St. Louis Rams, previously employed a running back named Lawrence Phillips, who is the same age as Chojnowski.

Here are a few of Mr. Phillips' youthful indiscretions:

- Stormed into a room occupied by his ex-girlfriend, grabbed her by the hair, dragged her down three flights of stairs, threw her against a wall and banged her head into a metal mailbox. He was given—ahem—probation. Shortly after that, St. Louis picked him in the first round of the NFL draft and signed him to a $5.6 million contract.
- Was convicted of drunk driving. How did the police notice? He was going 80 mph—with a flat tire.
- Was arrested at a party in Nebraska after two people said he assaulted them.
- Punched a woman in the face—knocking her unconscious, cutting her lip and chipping a tooth—at a Florida nightclub. Why? She refused to dance with him.

Sweet guy, huh? The Rams were not alone in hiring this idiot. The 49ers and Dolphins did, too.

The point is not the well-documented hypocrisy of the U.S.A.-loving, United Way-touting, "Hi Mom"-talking NFL. We have larger problems than that. One larger problem is that we've lost our collective mind.

That's the only possible explanation for our insistence on jailing people for what, in essence, is a personal-services agreement between two consenting adults.

Many of us believe prostitution is a sin. Fine. That's not the issue. There's a big difference between immoral and illegal. Or should be.

As I have noted before, when you compare Ms. Chojnowski's activities to other jobs in the service sector, singling out hookers makes no sense. To wit:

You can hire someone to clean your toilet.

You can hire someone to cook your dinner, then wash your dirty plates.

You can hire someone to scrape bubble gum off the floor of your car.

You can hire someone to trim your toenails.

You can hire someone to trim your mother's toenails.

You can hire someone to trim your dog's toenails.

You can hire someone to straighten your nose.

You can hire someone to stick little needles all over your body to try to ease your pain.

You can hire someone to poke a metal stud through your tongue or burn ink drawings onto your skin.

You can hire someone to put you on a couch, sort through your most intimate personal secrets and come up with a psychoanalysis.

You can hire someone to wade through your personal financial secrets and assemble your tax return.

You can hire someone to change your infant's poopy diapers.

You can hire someone to change your aging parent's poopy diapers.

You can hire people to dig weeds from your garden until their backs are breaking and their hands are blistered. And then they can hire someone to rub their back and feet. Or go to a high-priced "spa" and pay someone to rub mud on them.

But if you hire someone to rub one particular body part, you can be arrested, fined and jailed.

Actually, the contractor inevitably gets the worst of it. The guys in those little black books seem to skate away faster than Tara Lipinski on fresh ice.

The situation is even goofier in Summit County, where a prostitute is not merely a prostitute. In these parts, a prostitute is a ringleader of organized crime. Or so we have been told.

Fortunately, our top law-enforcers finally seem to be coming to their senses. Officials are talking about revisiting the Chojnowski case and related travesties. But as of this writing, Chojnowski is still facing 31 years in the slammer.

Lawrence Phillips, Attacker of Women, hasn't served 31 days.

We don't know how much tax money was spent on Summit County's ridiculous 18-month prostitution sting, and probably never will. Let's just call it a ton. There were limos to rent, fake offices to open, sex acts to buy—all with money that could have been spent nailing real criminals. People like, say, the second-most-important government official in Summit County, Bill Hartung, and his pal, county lawyer Cindy Peters, who were busy ripping off your tax money. Hartung and Peters together got less than one-tenth of Chojnowski's jail time.

And people say Ken Starr was overly aggressive. Ha! If President Clinton had done his cigar tricks in Summit County, he may have gotten the electric chair.

Jan. 30, 2000

Wimpy Texting Law Won't Keep Any of Us Safe

I will never figure out what most of those people are thinking in that stately building in Columbus where our laws are created.

Even after waiting until 43 other states had passed some type of law against texting while driving, the spineless weasels we elected have passed one of the nation's wimpiest texting laws, a law that will have virtually no impact on a growing threat to you and me and everyone we know and love.

Texting while driving a car is more dangerous than driving a car after pounding down a six-pack of beer.

A texting driver is *23 times* more likely to get into a crash than a non-texting driver. That comes from the highly respected Virginia Tech Transportation Institute.

That number is not some wild stab from a half-baked lab test. We're talking about multiple, large-scale, long-term, naturalistic driving studies that make use of sophisticated cameras and in-car instrumentation placed in the drivers' own cars.

Ohio's law, passed Tuesday and awaiting Gov. John Kasich's signature, will be little more than words on paper.

Why? Because for everyone over the age of 17, texting while driving will be a secondary offense, rather than a primary offense.

That means that if a cop drives right past you while your hand is on the wheel and your head is in your iPhone, he can't pull you over unless you have committed some other violation, such as running a red light.

Every citation written for texting will be paired with something else—most likely "failure to maintain assured clear distance." In other words, the texting ticket will be written after the texter rams into the back of some poor slob stopped at a traffic light.

Studies show that the average amount of time people take their eyes off the road while texting is five seconds. Now, that doesn't sound like a long period of time. But if you're going 65 miles per hour, in five seconds you cover the length of more than one and a half football fields.

Even if you're going only 25 mph, in five seconds you would travel 185 feet—a long, long way in city traffic.

Data collected by the Insurance Institute for Highway Safety shows that, of the 44 other states with texting laws, 36 make texting a primary violation for drivers of every age. But in Ohio, texting while driving is the legal equivalent of not wearing a seat belt.

Now, I don't drive half a mile without wearing a seat belt. But if you want to take the risk of flying through your windshield for no particular reason, that's your business. Too bad our elected officials can't tell the difference between a constituent killing himself and a constituent killing another constituent.

Some folks dismiss the value of texting laws by saying they'd be tough to enforce. Well, this one certainly will be. But if we allowed primary enforcement, the job would get a lot easier. I personally could have nailed five people in the past week.

Granted, I'm not driving a marked car. But the folks I saw were so preoccupied they wouldn't even notice a police cruiser. Hell, they wouldn't notice a flatbed trailer with monkeys jumping up and down singing *Who Let the Dogs Out?* to the accompaniment of the Ohio State Marching Band.

Why can't this state get anything right when it comes to driving? Our leaders consistently act as if raising the speed limit from 65 to 70 mph will result in mass carnage—ignoring the expertise of traffic engineers, who say the flow of traffic is far more important than the speed—but then go easy on a far bigger threat?

The reasons legislators have given for failing to support a serious texting law would be comical if they weren't so sad.

Proclaimed Sen. Bill Seitz of Cincinnati: "I make it a practice never to vote for a law that I might be guilty of."

Nice line. Awful viewpoint.

A state rep from northwest Ohio, Lynn Wachtmann, told the Toledo Blade he opposed the bill because "it's one of those basic freedom issues for me."

Are you kidding? You're complaining about incursions into your personal freedom in a state that permits sobriety checkpoints, where innocent motorists are pulled over at random by people in uniform carrying guns and are made to show their credentials, like residents of East Germany circa 1975?

If Kasich really thinks about this, he will put down his pen and send this piece of junk back to our legislators and tell them to get it right.

May 20, 2012

Troopers Launch Ticket-Writing Frenzy

The Ohio Highway Patrol is determined to bring safety to our interstates—even if it kills us.

All this week, packs of Columbus-based officers on white motorcycles have been prowling Akron's freeways, handing out tickets faster than a political candidate distributing fliers at a football game.

During the first three days alone: 600 citations.

At best, this is dirty pool. At worst, it is dangerous.

Dirty pool? Absolutely. Many of those tickets have been written on the recently revamped stretch of Interstate 77 that runs from Copley Road to the northern city limits.

As I reported in February, the speed limit on that new segment is now inappropriately low—so much so that the Ohio Department of Transportation has been trying to raise it from 55 mph to 65.

Thus far, those efforts have failed because of a quirk in a 1996 law that made 65 mph the default on Ohio's interstates. We'll spare you the gory details, which were reported earlier, but suffice it to say ODOT believes the 55-mph signs left over from the pre-widening days are outdated in the wake of the $64 million widening project completed late last year.

Today, the West Leg of the Akron Expressway might be the nicest, safest stretch of urban freeway in the entire state. It features three flat, straight, wide lanes in each direction, enormous berms and a stout concrete median.

So here we are, stuck with an artificially low speed limit, and where does the Ohio Highway Patrol choose to unleash a ticket-writing frenzy?

Although the patrol insists almost all of the tickets have been written for "aggressive violations"—defined as 20 mph or more over the limit— at least one Beacon Journal reader was ticketed for going 70 mph in a zone that clearly should be 65.

Even worse than picayune tickets is the added danger—for motorists *and* troopers.

Any traffic-safety expert in the land will tell you that the flow of traffic is more important than the speed. The most dangerous highways are those where drivers are traveling at radically different rates of speed.

It doesn't get much more radical than a pack of 70-mph drivers jamming their brakes to the floorboard the instant they spot a trooper on a motorcycle on the inside berm—much less five or six of them in the same area.

When reader Norma Shaub spotted a gaggle of troopers wedged between the left lane and the concrete median, "my first thought was, 'Are they crazy?' and my second thought was, 'How could anyone think this is a good idea?'

"They were pulling cars over onto the same shoulder by stepping out—in one case into the high-speed lane—and motioning for the vehicle to pull over! There are so many ways this could go so wrong."

A Beacon Journal employee saw a civilian motorcyclist who had been pulled over actually standing in the left lane. "The event almost caused one big accident," she said.

Reader Randy Adair said he witnessed two near-crashes in a single day. In one case, he said, a trooper aiming a laser gun had his hands extended into the left lane, causing a person in that lane to abruptly move to the center lane, nearly hitting another car, whose driver slammed on the brakes.

"I'm not a speeder," Adair said. "I set my cruise control at two or three miles under the limit. So that's not the issue."

The issue, he says, is that the officers are "not using their heads. They're jeopardizing the city of Akron in the name of protecting us, and, frankly, I don't need this much protection.

"There's a difference between protection and oppression, and it's not a helluva lot if it's carried too far."

As if you couldn't guess, the Highway Patrol takes a somewhat different view of things.

Lt. Eric Sheppard, from the patrol's Summit-Stark post, said he was not aware of ODOT's quest to raise the speed limit on the West Leg.

"I will tell you that about 98 percent of the citations that have been written are what we consider aggressive violations, which are at least 20 mph over the posted speed limit, which means even if it was at 65, they would be well in excess of the posted speed limit."

The patrol also has been working its magic on Interstates 76 and 277 and state Route 8.

Eight troopers are writing tickets for nine hours a day as part of a campaign known as Operation Clean Sweep. They started Monday and will finish Saturday—with luck, in one piece.

"These officers work urban highways nine months out of the year and they are very well aware of the safety concerns," Sheppard said, "and they are not going to place themselves or a violator in what they consider to be a hazardous situation."

Apparently, "hazardous" is very much in the eye of the beholder.

Akron's interstates have not experienced an upsurge in crashes. Rather, said Sheppard, "it has become a custom up there that the normal flow of traffic is well in excess of the posted speed limit, hence the safety reason of why we need to be up there and make a visible presence to try to change their driving behaviors."

Even the behavior-modification element is questionable. As reader Richard Zelin notes, "as soon as the patrol leaves the area, drivers will go back to driving above the limit."

That's not because Akron drivers are maniacal speed freaks. That's because national traffic experts say 85 percent of all motorists drive at a reasonable speed for the conditions regardless of the posted limit.

The patrol's Sheppard said he was not aware of studies that show traffic flow is a bigger safety factor than speed.

Well, for starters, he could check with the Federal Highway Administration. That group—not exactly a coalition of anarchists—spells out its speed-limit theory in Section 2B.13 of its Manual on Uniform Traffic Control Devices: "When a speed limit is to be posted, it should be within 5 mph of the 85th-percentile speed of free-flowing traffic."

That information is important in view of an FHA study identified as RD-85/096: "Speed zoning incorrectly used on streets and highways can lead to driver non-compliance with speed limits.

"[Matching the speed limit to the 85th percentile] results in speed limits that are not only acceptable to a large majority of the motorists, but also fall within the speed range where accident risk is lowest."

In other words, slower isn't necessarily better.

Would you rather be driving next to someone who is passing you at 70 mph or someone who is jamming on his brakes and veering into your lane because he has spotted four state troopers on the inside berm?

May 8, 2009

Ticket Binge on I-77 Pays the Bills

Did you hear a jingling sound on the Akron Expressway a couple of weeks ago?

That wasn't a pebble stuck in your hubcap. That was the city of Akron and the state of Ohio hitting the jackpot.

From May 4 through May 8, eight motorcycle cops imported from the Columbus post of the State Highway Patrol wrote 733 speeding tickets.

The total take for that five-day Expressway binge: $103,902.

When the patrol writes a speeding ticket in Akron, the city gets 40 percent of the fine money, the county gets 10 percent and the state walks away with 50 percent.

Akron also gets 62 percent of the court costs, with Ohio taking the rest.

Of those 733 tickets, 66 percent were written on the West Leg, between Copley Road and Ridgewood Road—the same stretch of Interstate 77 where the Ohio Department of Transportation says the speed limit is too low.

As we first reported four months ago, ODOT is trying to raise the limit there from 55 mph to 65 in the wake of a $64 million construction project that widened the West Leg to three lanes in each direction.

Although the patrol has claimed that "about 98 percent" of the tickets it wrote that week were handed to people committing "aggressive violations," a Beacon Journal analysis of the tickets shows that only 51 percent could even remotely be said to fit that description.

In Akron Municipal Court, where all of these tickets wound up, speed violations are separated into three categories. The more you exceed the limit, the more you pay. Here is the breakdown:

- Up to 15 mph over the limit: $119 (including court costs).
- From 16 to 20 mph over the limit: $124.
- More than 20 mph over the limit: $159.

During the patrol's blitz, 49 percent of all the tickets written on all legs of the Akron Expressway were for 20 mph or lower.

So much for targeting maniacs. How "aggressive" can somebody be if he doesn't even fall into the court's highest fine category?

And remember that 65 percent of those tickets were written in a zone that should be 10 mph faster—if not 15 mph faster.

As you may have read, two state representatives this week introduced a bill to raise the speed limit on Ohio's interstates to 70.

Ohio's speed limits are the lowest in America. Fully two-thirds of the lower 48 states have speed limits of 70 mph or above. In 12 states, the limit is 75.

Granted, Ohio doesn't have a lot in common geographically with many of the 75-mph states, such as Arizona, Texas and Colorado. But we have quite a bit in common with Indiana, Michigan, West Virginia and Kentucky. In those four states—all of which touch our border—the speed limit on interstates is 70.

Why is 70 safe in Indiana and Michigan but unsafe in Ohio?

It's not. But keeping the speed limit low makes it easier for governmental entities to use our freeways as ATMs.

The idea that most speed enforcement is designed to enhance public safety rather than generate money is laughable. In most cases, speed traps do little more than create a hidden tax. And this latest unauthorized tax collection may have been unprecedented.

So many tickets were written that the clerk of courts office, which operates 24 hours a day, was overrun. During the second and third shifts, workers from the criminal division were loaned to the traffic division to try to keep pace with the paperwork.

Scott Gale, chief deputy clerk of courts, said this was the biggest ticket-writing frenzy he can remember during his 12 years with the court.

Anybody else think the heart of a recession is not the best time to add to the financial burden of 733 households?

Paying for a traffic violation in Ohio is even worse than buying a concert ticket from Ticketmaster, where a "$37" ticket ends up costing $47.50 after an "admission" fee and a "convenience" fee are tacked on.

In Akron, if your speeding fine is, say, $29 (the lowest category), you have to add another $90 for "court costs."

Of that, $34 is mandated by the state. Ohio takes money for

victims of crime, the public defender, drug-law enforcement, an indigent driver alcohol treatment fund and an "indigent defense support fund." (Why a speeder should help pay for such things as drug enforcement and alcohol treatment is beyond me, but that's a topic for another day.)

Akron keeps 62 percent of the court costs: $7 for the computerization of records, $2 for "bank automation" (such as processing credit card payments), $32 for "basic costs" (everything else associated with running the court, from salaries to wastebaskets) and $15 for a "special projects fund." The latter is a fancy way of saying "slush fund."

"Special projects" are essentially anything the judges want that's not already covered. If you were nailed with a speeding ticket during the past several years in northeast Summit County, where the Cuyahoga Falls Municipal Court had jurisdiction, you paid a $20 special projects fee and personally helped finance the new $9 million courthouse in Stow.

No wonder a recent study by a panel of state legislators, judges, lawyers and others concluded that court costs are out of control.

"The General Assembly [should] amend the statutes to clarify what these 'special project' funds can be used for," the panel wrote.

"It should be made clear that these funds are not intended to completely fund the construction . . . of court facilities, nor serve as a permanent substitute for general funding."

Anybody still think speeding tickets are all about safety?

Look, we're not lobbying for the Akron Grand Prix. We're just looking for speeds that are reasonable for the conditions.

And we'd also like to know our tax rate up front.

May 22, 2009

Arrogance of Feds Unites Unlikely Pair

There's a local militia guy who keeps sending me long, unsigned, hate-filled letters.

The latest batch was triggered by the trial of Oklahoma City bombing suspect Tim McVeigh. One missive blames the bombing on "rogue elements of the U.S. government."

You've probably heard about these militia types. But you may not realize they have something in common with one of Akron's most prominent businessmen.

By any of the traditional yardsticks, Russ Vernon is an American success story.

Since taking over West Point Market in 1960, he has expanded seven times and turned the specialty food store into a nationally recognized operation.

Vernon's cheese department has been called one of the 10 best in the country by Esquire magazine. The author of a book called *On Great Service* calls West Point "the finest retail store I have encountered in 28 years of teaching and studying."

Vernon would seem to have compelling reasons to want to preserve the political status quo. But just like my militia guy, Vernon is deeply resentful of the massive power of the federal government—and thinks the country is headed for ruin unless fundamental changes are made.

Unlike my militia guy, Vernon—a tall, polite, intense man who wears wire-rim glasses and bow ties—doesn't have to settle for writing unsigned notes.

We have written extensively about his plight. And three weeks ago, the nation's largest newspaper, the Wall Street Journal, gave him space for a 1,000-word anti-Washington tirade.

Vernon is so well-connected that the governor writes letters on his behalf. Seriously. Gov. George Voinovich went to bat for him. And even that didn't help much.

Vernon's troubles began in 1991, when a local resident accused him of not hiring enough blacks.

Never mind that not one African-American applicant or employee had charged the store with discrimination. Never mind that the local chapter of the NAACP considered Vernon an ally and came to his defense.

The Equal Employment Opportunity Commission smelled a rat, so the EEOC went to work.

Based solely on the fact that only 5 percent of West Point's employees were black—not as high as the city's overall population—the EEOC said Vernon must have discriminated.

The agency said everyone would live happily ever after if West Point immediately imposed a 33 percent minority hiring quota and paid $100,000 to the 24 black applicants who hadn't been hired during the previous three years.

Remember, none of them had complained. In fact, two had been offered jobs but declined.

Despite letters from the Guv, the NAACP, Ohio's senators and others, the EEOC harassed Vernon for 30 months. Rescuing him literally required an act of Congress: a long-overdue law that enables small companies to be reimbursed for legal fees if they are unjustly prosecuted.

Wonder of wonders, the EEOC immediately backed off and settled for Vernon's longstanding offer to invite all 24 applicants to reapply; any who were hired and stayed for a year would get a $1,000 scholarship. Not one person reapplied.

Bottom line: "Minorities didn't get anything, the EEOC didn't get anything," says Vernon. "Only our attorney got something."

What if Vernon hadn't had $67,000 for legal fees? What if he weren't nationally known?

What if he were just some little guy minding his own store when the government swooped down to inflict, as he puts it, a "reign of terror"? Could you blame someone in that position for heading into the hills?

For the record, Vernon says he can't relate to the militia movement "because that's not the way things are done." But as he sits sipping coffee at the rear of his local landmark, he sounds an awful lot like a guy who would be tempted to sign up.

"How do you get rid of bureaucracy? It only gets bigger. This is a cancer that is affecting small business across the country, and I think it's not in our national interest not to address it."

Even federal bureaucrats should be smart enough to realize this: If you create enough Russ Vernons, you eventually create a revolution.

April 16, 1997

Idiot Candidates & a Pinheaded Editor

When the Beacon Journal invited the area's political candidates to submit their profiles for posting on Ohio.com, some fascinating responses rolled in.

A woman running for a suburban school board said she should be elected because she wanted to "polarize" the board. She was given an opportunity to consult a dictionary to make sure that's what she really meant.

A candidate for a city school board—spelled "B-O-R-D" in his e-mail—submitted a sales pitch that included a non-sensical sentence and three horrendous misspellings. He wanted to make the school system sufficiently "appelling" to "attrack" additional students.

Each candidate was allowed 70 words. A man running for a suburban city council turned in 247. Want to put him in charge of your budget?

I'd name these people, but I was ordered not to by the newspaper's managing editor, a pinheaded, pencil-necked, bean-counting geek from Green who sits in a nice office with a big window.

He said identifying these word butchers wouldn't be "fair." His lame rationale: Many of the nearly 600 candidates who have submitted profiles committed spelling and grammatical blunders, and the newspaper cleaned up some of those before posting them. So why single out just a few people for ridicule?

Because it would be fun, that's why.

Now, newspapers are not in the business of putting words in people's mouths, but we often clean up spelling errors in such things as letters to the editor. First of all, we don't want our readers to have to struggle to figure out what word the letter-writer really meant. Second, most of the people who write letters don't write for a living and can't be expected to know their way around every syllable in the dictionary. (Lord knows, we don't, either.)

However, when someone is running for an office that will enable him or her to influence the way in which we educate children, it is not unreasonable to expect basic literacy.

Were some of these misspellings merely typing errors? Doesn't matter. What kind of educator—or councilperson, for that matter—wouldn't bother to check his or her work before turning it in?

The good news: During the unsightly confrontation between your favorite columnist and his windbag editor, it came to light that the latter had actually contemplated posting all of the submissions exactly the way they came in—and we might just do so for the next election, in February.

So be forewarned, candidates: You spell it wrong, that's how it could stay.

You don't have to be a Rhodes Scholar to do a good job in public office. But you should be able to spell "public office."

And don't just rely on your computer's spell check. You could leave out the letter "L" in "public" and the word would sail right through. Then you'd *really* have issues.

Oct. 20, 2009

DOIN' STUFF

Next Bus Stop: Oblivion

Would I like to hop behind the wheel of a city bus and give it a spin?

Is Bill Gates solvent?

Now, I'll be the first to admit my bus-driving qualifications were suspect. My only connection to the bus company, in fact, was a column in which I made fun of the news that 75 Summit County buses will get satellite-controlled computers to automatically announce upcoming stops.

Did the bus honchos recoil in horror at my jabs? Did they consult the spinmeisters to try to discredit me? Nah. They laughed. Then they tossed me their keys.

Is this a great country or what?

The invitation came in the form of a letter from Metro Regional Transit Authority's top kahuna, Robert Pfaff, who offered what he termed "a free bus-driving lesson—off road, of course."

Off-road bus driving? Now that's the coolest thing I've ever heard! You mean I can drive it up the side of mountains and through rivers and over boulders and—what? Oh. You just meant off the street?

Well, that's OK, too. For a guy whose idea of a "big rig" is the family minivan, the chance to commandeer a 40-foot-long, 20-ton, $250,000 amalgamation of metal sounds like a little piece of internal-combustion heaven.

Granted, a city bus' zero-to-60 time won't accelerate the heart rate. And those paint jobs wouldn't get you very far in the free-market showroom. But how can you turn down the chance to attach your right foot to a 285-horse engine getting less than 6 miles per gallon?

A female colleague—in an effort to protect her privacy, we shall refer to her simply as "Sheryl Harris"—caught wind of this invitation and asked, in an edgy sort of way, if this were a childhood fantasy come true.

The implication, of course, was that this is further evidence of some deep-seated need found only in people with a Y chromosome. A dreaded Guy Thing. Perhaps the ultimate Guy Thing, in which the Tim "Tool Time" Allen mentality is pushed to the edge of the envelope.

Nah. This is not a childhood fantasy. It's an adult fantasy. The older I get, in fact, the more my thoughts turn to gigantic machines.

My ultimate fantasy, since you asked, is—OK, let me qualify that: My ultimate *vehicular* fantasy—involves a huge, loud, smelly, dirty, dented, smoking, earth-moving machine. Tires the size of Mogadore. Tall and shapely, with a cab so big you could put a refrigerator in it. Big enough to mow down a small mountain with one swipe. Or at least a hill. Maybe Chapel Hill. Yeah! Drive it through Chapel Hill Mall, right down the concourse, ramming through kiosks, terrorizing shoppers, having my way with our arrogant, pointless, consumer-obsessed society.

But we digress.

We were heading to the bus garage near Summit Lake in Akron.

My first impression is not encouraging. At the entrance to the facility is a big sign saying, "11 Days Without An Accident." As if they're talking millennia.

Now, rearranging things with earth-moving equipment is one thing. But my impression, as a layman, has always been that one of the chief goals in bus driving is to avoid stuff.

Wrong, crankshaft breath. The primary goal of bus driving, I am told, does not even involve driving.

"You talk about empowerment!" says Andy Ervin, a 22-year Metro veteran. "This is a true job for empowerment! This is a great job!"

Ervin talks like that all the time. He's cheerful, peppy and encouraging. Which he damn well better be, because part of his job involves training new drivers.

He teaches them that the actual driving is just part of the equation. The biggest task is dealing with the public.

Although Ervin is a trusting soul, he is not trusting enough to turn over the controls until we get to the mammoth parking lot of the Akron Baptist Temple, where he sets up a number of plastic pylons.

Then he surrenders my machine—No. 1011, as I affectionately refer to it. It's a 1997 Nova, manufactured in, believe it or not, Roswell, New Mexico (insert creepy music here).

I quickly absorb the basics, including the odd transmission— neither on the stick nor the floor, it's a push-button deal to the driver's left. And soon I am privy to the whole secret of driving a bus: developing a close personal relationship with your rearview mirrors. Or, as Ervin puts it: "Trust the Force."

I did, and the Force was with me. Well, most of the time.

Although the Force shorted out momentarily during the later stages, I prefer to look upon the bright side: During my initial slalom run through pylons, I ran over only one "pedestrian." And I actually backed through the entire course without hitting a thing.

Finally, the ultimate achievement: Parallel parked the beast on my first try, without so much as a dented fender.

Then I got cocky.

Ervin moved the slalom cones closer together—36 feet. Apparently a 40-foot bus doing a quick weave will not successfully clear cones that are 36 feet apart. My wake looked like Hurricane Andrew's. But a second try, with wider sweeps, was successful.

Ervin was relentlessly complimentary. Even after my cavalier slalom run in which the death toll reached 7, he yelled, "Didn't miss by much!"

He said I definitely would have been invited back for more training—in contrast to the 13 percent who wash out immediately.

Prospective drivers (who, if hired, earn about $16 an hour) are put through a seven-week program, of which driving is just a small part. Perhaps it should come as no surprise that the training for prospective bus drivers includes megadoses of stress management, complete with breathing techniques and visualization.

Well, Andy, I've been practicing my visualization. But I've gotta tell you: My visions still seem to involve earth-moving equipment.

June 5, 1998

Out of the Way, Casey Jones

"Phallic," muttered my female editor.

"You're pitiful," taunted a female reporter.

OK, so it is a guy thing. Tough noogies. I'm a guy. Live with it. In fact, get comfortable with it. This may develop into a long-running series.

First, a man calls me up and asks whether I want to drive a city bus. Then another guy reads my bus column and calls to ask whether I want to drive a locomotive. Not a Lionel. A real locomotive. A 126-ton, horn-blaring, track-eating hunk of diesel-fired heavy metal.

Aaaaahhhrrrrrrrr.

The call came from a fellow who works with a fellow who employs an engineer. The engineer does his thing for Portage Limestone on the southwest outskirts of Kent.

"The thing about railroading is, it's still an adventure," says Bob, the engineer. Bob doesn't want his last name used—probably, as you will see later, for good reason.

"If you want to go someplace and just get there, fly. But if you want an adventure, go by train. . . . [Having this job] is like being touched by an angel."

He really said that. I have witnesses.

The angelic locomotive only plies a two-mile stretch of track. It picks up cars filled with stone near Mogadore Road and yanks them back toward Middlebury Road in the heart of the 15-acre Portage Limestone complex, where the contents are dumped into a pit and then stacked in temporary gray mountains. But despite the shortness of the run—done at a top speed of 10 mph—"it's still an adventure," insists Bob.

Bob is right on. Now level with me: Could you pass up the chance to drive a metallic beast that, when fully loaded with 45 cars, gets 8 gallons per mile? That's not MPG, mind you; we're talking GPM.

RRRRRRrrrrr.

In railroad parlance, my engine is a GT-10. She's medium blue with white trim. Yes, she.

"All good pieces of equipment are named after women because they have their own peculiarities," proclaims Bob. His boss, Herbert Hirt, rolls his eyes and moans at the political incorrectness.

"They do!" says Bob. "They have a personality. They could be identically built, but they still have their own personality."

My heavy-metal babe, known to her friends as No. 7564, once had a fling with Conrail. The offspring of General Motors employees, she was born in 1955—and looks marvelous for her age.

"These are made to last forever, barring a catastrophic event," says Bob, making what I hoped was not an allusion to my impending run. "The technology changes are what makes them obsolete. This uses 5½ gallons an hour just sitting here idling; the new ones maybe 3."

Before we get started, Bob informs me, we always walk around the train to make sure nobody's sleeping under it. Apparently, people who would never dream of sleeping under an auto are drawn to trains.

Then Bob shows me what's under the hood. Make that *hoods*. He opens and closes a series of heavy vertical doors that hide an endless parade of greasy metal stuff.

"It has its own starter coil," Bob tells me.

"These are the decompression plugs," Bob tells me.

My eyes glaze over. Suddenly, I'm flashing back to adolescence, when my father repeatedly attempted to show me how to maintain and repair the family cars. At least that's what he said he was doing. Actually, he just needed someone to hold the light. From age 11 to 18, I thought my name was "Hold The Light, Will Ya?" I never actually fixed anything. My ultimate goal was simply to avoid casting shadows onto the wrong gizmo.

"We're starting to prime the engine," Bob is telling me as I return from my flashback. Then he begins babbling about pressurization.

Compared to driving a bus, driving a train is rocket science. There are levers and dials and handles and foot pedals as far as the eye can see. You can brake with the engine brake or the train brake. Then there's the big red "full emergency" lever. (I make a special effort to remember that one.) By the time Bob says, "The next thing we're gonna do is energize your generator field," my head is ready to explode.

Energize my generator field? What is this, *Star Wars*?

But energize we did, and soon I'm reveling in raw power. You should hear this sucker.

Firing up an 1,800-horsepower diesel-electric locomotive is like putting on the headphones, turning the treble all the way down and maxing out the bass and volume.

And talk about bells and whistles! The bell—triggered by pulling out a brass lever—is cool enough. But when you pull on the air horn . . . guy nirvana. The horn is audible five miles away. You can blast it over and over. In fact, as you approach an intersection, railroad etiquette requires two long blasts, one short blast and another long blast. You honk once before stopping . . . twice before moving forward . . . three times before backing up . . . four times to call the brakeman from the east . . . five times to call the brakeman from the west.

You use a series of short blasts to express "concern." (Another good thing to remember.)

And then, apparently, you can occasionally honk just for the hell of it. Which I did. A lot.

I drove about a mile down the track, shockingly close to downtown Kent, crossing over actual, working intersections. *Hoooonk.* Then I reversed the engine and backed up almost two miles, passing our original starting point and heading onto a rarely-traveled stretch of track, a stretch used only to store cars. Because it doesn't get much action, tall weeds have grown up through the rails and tree branches have encroached into the airspace.

Railroads use a lot of weed killer. Although weeds are no match for a 126-ton locomotive, they make the track slippery and are tough to pry off the metal wheels. Or, as Bob so eloquently puts it, "Weeds are like snot on a doorknob." You sure you don't want your last name used?

Anyway, a good time was had by all, with the possible exception of a female onlooker, who seemed more disturbed than I when Bob commented that, in real life, I would have been fired for exceeding the 10 mph speed limit by 8 mph. She also seemed less amused than the rest of us when the train clobbered a series of tree branches. Apparently, membership in her gender prohibits her from fully appreciating destruction done solely for the sake of destruction.

What's next? Well, having passed my locomotive-driving test, more or less, Herb said he could probably get me into the cab of a long-distance train that hits 60 mph. He also gave me the name of a guy who owns gigantic earthmoving equipment.

So the future looks bright. The ceiling is unlimited. Full speed ahead.

And, remember, my phone number appears at the end of this column. Any unreasonable offer will be considered.

Sept. 16, 1998

Thundering Through the Corn

WEST SALEM: They first started racing in this big ol' Wayne County cornfield in 1958—and not much has changed. The boys still gather several times a week to go head-to-head in their souped-up cars, to inhale cigarettes and gasoline fumes and exhale the worries and restraints of everyday life.

Dragway 42 boils down to two lanes of blacktop. It's machine vs. machine. Gearhead versus gearhead. The only thing missing is John Travolta dancing with Olivia Newton-John.

Well, that and my stomach. Thanks to a lunatic named Gene Kirby, my stomach is now located somewhere behind my vertebrae. That's what happens when you go from 0 to 123 mph in a quarter of a mile.

Longest 11 seconds of my life.

Kirby, who lives in Cuyahoga Falls, isn't much of a host. He couldn't even offer me a passenger's seat. Yanked the sucker out a long time ago so he could reduce the weight and go faster. Took about everything else out, too, until his 1984 Pontiac Grand Prix became essentially a gigantic engine on wheels. So I had to sit on the metal floor and clutch the roll cage in a state of sustained panic as he rocketed down the asphalt to a sonic accompaniment that resembled a perpetual explosion.

And nobody even asked me to sign a waiver! Man, this place really is 1958.

But I figured my chances of survival were at least 50-50. Kirby has been doing this for a long, long time. Started going to the track at age 6 with his older brother. He's 43 now and has raced all over the place for decades.

Besides, what could possibly go wrong? Well, yeah, a few years ago a guy got going so fast that he flew right off the end of the runway, went airborne over the little rural road that divides southern Medina County from northern Wayne, and wound up dead in a field. And, yeah, earlier this season a motorcycle racer lost a foot when he slammed into the guardrail.

And, OK, just last month Gene's own machine burst into flames when he blew out the transmission at the starting line.

"I got it off to the side and got the fire out," he says. "Two days later I had it all back together." No big deal.

But if you think Kirby's wheels are missing a few ball bearings, so to speak, what about the judgment of his good pal, Bob Dove? Imagine this: Dove, who has operated Dove Auto Body in the Falls since 1974, actually let me run his dragster.

Really. After giving me a 10-minute crash course (oops, poor choice of words), Dove sent me out on the blacktop to put his pride and joy—a juiced-up 1964 Plymouth Barracuda—through actual time trials.

What a trip! Heck, I'd have been delighted just to "burn the tires," a move that surely was invented by somebody who was looking for a way to get back at his driver-education teacher.

To do a burn, you plant your left foot firmly on the brake pedal, stomp on the accelerator with your right foot and breathe deeply as the cabin fills with smoke from your tires. In addition to delighting tire manufacturers, this little maneuver heats up the rubber so the car gets better traction. You don't want to hang around the starting line spinning your wheels while the guy in the next lane is roaring down the track.

The start is everything. (Well, shifting into the right gears helps, too, but we'll get to that in a minute.) As you pull your car up next to the "Christmas tree," a pole with colored lights that controls the start, you creep toward an electronic eye. When your front tires hit the proper spot, a double yellow light glows on the tree. Then, even more slowly, you edge forward to a second electronic eye, which triggers another double yellow light. When both cars are in that position, the countdown begins.

You get a big yellow light, then another, then a third. The instant the third light comes on, you initiate your blastoff in anticipation of the green light that follows. But if you leave a hair too soon, you get the dreaded red light—a foul.

Fouling is a serious problem. We're not talking about free throws here. In an actual drag race, we're talking about instant defeat. And in time trials, we're talking about a clocking that doesn't count.

Now, compared to Kirby's car, Dove's gold Barracuda is a tricycle. Kirby's Grand Prix uses 7 gallons of fuel per mile and has to be carted around on a trailer because it isn't street legal.

Dove drives his 'Cuda back and forth to work each day. If you saw it in a parking lot, you'd never dream it could turn the quarter-mile in as little as 15½ seconds. And it even has a passenger's seat.

Still, as Dove climbed into that passenger's seat and I drove toward the starting line for the first time, my eyes were bigger than Little Orphan Annie's.

Double yellow. Double yellow. Yellow . . . yellow . . . yellow—go!

Dove would later call my reaction time—.570 seconds, according to the computer printout given to each racer after a run—"real good. Better than mine."

I roared down the track in first gear, one eye on the road, the other on the tachometer mounted down by the gearshift. The special gearshift looks like an automatic—unlike the "H" shifting pattern in a normal car, these gears are in a straight line, and there's no clutch.

But you're supposed to shift forward each time the tach gets to the red line. Which is exactly what I did—except I pushed the stick a tad too far and shifted from first into third. Not good.

Immediately I realized my mistake, downshifted to second and completed the run in semicompetent fashion. But the damage had been done, competitively speaking. I finished with a lame 16.5 seconds and a top speed of 85 mph.

Much to my astonishment, the easygoing Dove declared me ready to solo. "I'm gonna get a cup of coffee," he said, climbing out. Then he pointed to his cell phone and laughed. "If you need help, here's the phone."

Fortunately, all of this madness takes place in the middle of nowhere. Dragway 42 is so isolated, in fact, that when Jack Ehrmantaut bought the place in 1991, he had to match an offer from a garbage company that was preparing to convert it to a landfill.

Ehrmantaut had raced professionally all over the country and was ready to put down roots. But he wasn't ready to give up his first love.

"It's a personal challenge to see how good you can get," he says of the sport. "And it's competitive. You're trying to beat the other guy."

But you're not trying to beat the law. Notes Jack's son, Toby: "The racers can take their cars out and see how fast they can go without worrying about the cops."

Race down that runway just once and you can fully understand the appeal. Time slows to a crawl. Your senses come alive. There's just the right touch of danger. Well, more than the right touch. In fact, I haven't been this scared since I had to drive through the Tallmadge Circle.

On my second run, I was determined to block everything out and combine a quick start with the proper shifting. And I did. Started so fast, in fact, that I fouled. But, hey, I cut more than half a second off my time and hit 86 mph. Foul, schmoul.

On my final run, wary of fouling again, I held back a bit and logged a reaction time of .660. But that was good enough to win. Yep, I actually beat somebody! Zoomed across the finish line in 16.2, more than a second better than my opponent. (OK, he was driving a pickup truck. But we don't need to dwell on that.)

And so, loyal readers, we're on a roll. In June, I was invited to drive a city bus; went around plastic pylons at 5 mph. In August, I was invited to drive a freight train; went down the rails at 20 mph. Now I'm drag-racing at 86 mph.

Maybe we should call a halt to this before it gets completely out of hand. If I go any faster, I'll be airborne.

Speaking of which . . . I've always wondered what it would be like to pilot the Goodyear blimp. Not that I'm trying to drop a hint or anything.

Oct. 11, 1998

Blimp Pilot Terrorizes Akron

If you spotted the Goodyear blimp over Akron the other day and wondered why it was swaying wildly back and forth, wonder no more.

Capt. Dyer reporting for duty.

Seriously. My wildest dream. Your worst nightmare.

After driving a city bus, a locomotive and a dragster, I dropped a printed hint about the blimp—and a couple days later my phone rang with an invitation.

Which begs the question: What's *wrong* with you people? I have no qualifications for any of this! All I can do is type! What are you thinking?!

But we digress.

We were talking about how the $5 million Spirit of Akron—the biggest, fastest airship in Goodyear's fleet—came to be flopping around in the autumn sky like a giant maple leaf that had surrendered its hold on a tree. It's a wonder nobody called 1-800-GRAB-DUI.

Let the record show that the guest pilot was stone-cold sober. The problem was, um, the wind. Yeah, that's it. The wind. It was blowing at 18 mph. Funny thing, though—the blimp didn't seem to shake, rattle and roll while the regular pilot was in command.

If Capt. John Moran was having second thoughts about turning over his controls to a novice, he did a great job of disguising it. I'm pretty sure that tortured voice I heard—"The humanity! The humanity!"—was coming from inside my own head.

Fortunately, unlike the hydrogen-filled Hindenburg, the Spirit of Akron is not a tinderbox.

Blimp builders long ago learned their lesson: Although hydrogen provides better lift and is more readily available, helium makes a lot more sense because it's very stable, with a slow reaction rate. That's what I kept telling myself as I tried to chase away visions of infernos.

Get a grip, boy! How much trouble can you get into going 35 mph? Have you ever read a news report about a "low-speed crash"? Heck, you've gone this fast on water skis!

Then I tried this: You live on a planet that is spinning around at 1,040 mph while it moves through space at 66,600 mph. How much scarier can things get?

Well, pretty scary. This 205-foot-long floating billboard is made out of polyester, for god's sake—polyester fabric backed with a thin coat of neoprene. And it has two ropes dangling from its nose, like a birthday balloon whose owner lost her grip.

Apparently, the tension was visible on my face because Moran told me to relax. Now, Moran has been flying blimps for 30 years and is widely considered the best in the world. For a big sports telecast, he will take the Spirit up in weather conditions nobody else would dream of challenging. And, according to Moran, one of the keys to being a successful pilot is to act like everything is under control— even when it's not. Especially when it's not.

That would have required more acting ability than I possess. But I took a big breath and tried to enjoy myself as we soared clumsily over Springfield Lake, heading toward Derby Downs and the Rubber Bowl.

"It's just like the joystick on your computer," Moran was saying.

Well, it does look the same. But if this were a computer game, I'd return it to the store.

You push the stick right . . . take a nap . . . get a snack . . . read the paper . . . and maybe by then the blimp will move to the right. While you're waiting, you flop the stick around, trying to generate some kind of action. And eventually you do. But by then you're a few steps behind. Or ahead. I still haven't quite figured it out. Let's just say this thing ain't exactly equipped with rack-and-pinion steering.

The blimp surged right, the blimp surged left. Beacon Journal photographer Ed Suba was flopping around the inside of the gondola like a goldfish on a countertop.

I must say I felt considerably better a few days later when I logged onto Goodyear's website and read the list of "frequently asked questions"—specifically, "What is it like to fly the blimp?"

"The blimp has a life of its own in the air. Its movements are slow and ponderous, and yet it reacts very intimately to air currents and thermals. It can take several seconds for the ship to respond to the pilot's commands, and as a result, blimp pilots (must) develop a feel that helps them counteract the blimp's inclination to aimless meanderings."

Boy, they got that right. Aimless Meanderings R Us.

But one direction seems to require very little coaxing—down. Down works. You push down, it goes down.

One of my best downward surges came as we approached the Rubber Bowl at the precise moment a University of Akron football game was ending. The players and fans must have flashed back to the movie *Black Sunday*.

Our plunge took place shortly after the pilot said we were a little too high, that I should bring it down from 2,500 to 2,000 feet. He probably didn't mean all at once. But what do you want from a rookie?

Part of the problem is that when you think you're flying level, you're actually going up.

That's why a greenhorn needs to keep a close eye on the altimeter. (Please note my facile use of pilot jargon.) Most of the time we stayed between 1,000 and 2,000 feet. The Spirit of Akron is capable of cruising at 10,000 feet and 65 mph, but that defeats the purpose. The whole idea is to promote Goodyear. If nobody can read the big yellow-and-blue "No. 1 in Tires" logo on the side, the company is wasting a whole bunch of money.

So rid your mind of any salacious thoughts about the Mile High Club. The best a couple could do in the blimp is the Quarter-Mile High Club.

Actually, blimps are no laughing matter at Goodyear. The company spends $18 million a year to keep its six airships aloft. In addition to the Spirit, based at Wingfoot Lake in Portage County, there's the Eagle in Los Angeles and the Stars and Stripes in Pompano Beach, Fla.

Three smaller ships carry the Goodyear message in Europe and South America.

As you may have guessed, piloting a blimp is not exactly a mainstream career path. Each of the Goodyear's six ships has four pilots. Do the math, bucko.

"When Goodyear needs a blimp pilot, we go out and hire an airplane pilot and teach them how to fly the blimp," Moran said over the hum of two 425-horsepower turboprops attached to the side of the gondola.

I always figured you had to manipulate the helium to go up and down, like a hot-air balloon changes its air temperature. But basically you just drive the thing up and drive it back down.

In the hands of a professional, the ride is incredibly smooth, even on a day with moderate wind. Moran says that smoothness is the biggest surprise for most first-time riders.

The big bird also is surprisingly plush. I expected the inside to resemble a glorified school bus. Instead, it's more like a private jet, with a single row of comfortable cloth seats on either side of a center aisle.

The Spirit of Akron has eight passenger seats, but the normal limit is six. It's based not only on air temperature but the weight of the passengers—which, as you can image, has led to an occasional ugly scene at the ol' loading dock.

The pilots' seats are sandwiched around enough computer and electronic equipment to intimidate George Lucas. But operating the blimp requires an odd combination of high-tech equipment and good, old-fashioned muscle.

On the landing—the trickiest part—the pilot guns the blimp down hard, directly into the wind, and two guys on the ground catch the ropes and hold on for dear life. Then, half a million other guys in blue jumpsuits run up and grab on to the sides of the gondola to keep it near the ground.

Actually, 13 people are required for each takeoff and landing. When the wind is blowing, two of them look like characters in an old silent movie: As the blimp rolls around in the wind on its one retractable wheel, they chase it around with a portable yellow ladder. Just as they are about to hook the ladder on, the wind changes direction and the blimp floats away again.

This can continue for quite some time. On most days, the big bag of helium never comes to a full stop.

But this funky boarding procedure just makes the blimp that much more lovable. This is a magical machine, a klutzy, endearing behemoth that, in the words of one Goodyear employee, is like "a giant, puffy grandmother."

Because Puff Granny is so much slower than an airplane, you can not only see the passing panorama, but really study it . . . the little cars moving through their blacktopped maze . . . the ripples spreading out and fading on the area's many lakes . . . the leisurely movement of birds' wings as they soar below you.

Granny also has magical bloodlines. Her Wingfoot Lake hangar dates all the way back to World War I, when Goodyear cranked out 1,000 balloons and 100 airships for the Allies.

The last military airship was delivered to the Navy in 1962. Since then, the blimps have been strictly a PR gimmick. Their only real mission is to thrill.

Mission accomplished.

Nov. 18, 1998

Killing the Coliseum

Architects inhabit the realm of poets and painters. They take blank slates and create something from nothing. The best of them, on their best days, produce work that seems to involve the hand of God.

Craig Webb lives in a different realm. On his best days, the results seem to mirror the backhand of God. He has more in common with tornadoes and earthquakes.

But devolution has its rewards. I can now speak from firsthand experience. At a time of year when colleges are handing out honorary degrees, Webb has bestowed upon me a particularly rare and coveted title: Doctor of Destruction.

Late last month, Webb and his boss, Bobby DiGeronimo of Independence Excavating, let me climb into the cab of a 150-foot crane, tee up a 6,000-pound wrecking ball and smash it into the last remnants of the Richfield Coliseum.

Yeah, it's another one of those guy things. What's the point of being a guy if you can't trash stuff using gigantic machines? And I'm here to tell you that life just doesn't get any better than blasting a 3-ton sphere of steel against the side of a local landmark.

The unfortunate irony is that I loved that place.

When the carpetbaggers from Cleveland stole the Cavaliers and the concerts and the circus and all the other fun stuff, leaving the 20-year-old Coliseum without a mission, I was sick. I still think it was a sin to spend $150 million in tax money to duplicate a perfectly good arena.

Actually, the clowns in Cleveland didn't even duplicate it. For $150 million, they gave us an inferior building. The sightlines at Gund Arena are terrible. The seats are too close together. The lack of an interior concourse makes you feel as if you've been stuffed into a closet—and reinforces the notion of a caste system based on ticket price. Even the color scheme is lame.

Not that this 5-year-old development still bothers me. Not a chance.

OK, maybe I did feel the need for a little therapy. And nothing lifts the spirit like a little controlled aggression.

In honor of the occasion, I donned an old Cleveland Cavaliers T-shirt. Real old. Back to the Miracle of Richfield era—the wine-and-gold colors with that little Cavalier guy holding a sword.

Slaying this beast would take more than a sword, though. Webb and his pals had been trying to knock it down for more than two months. When a building is reared on reinforced concrete and massive steel beams, it doesn't surrender without a fight.

Craig Webb has been fighting such fights for more than half of his 45 years. The thrill is nearly gone.

"There's always that little adrenalin rush," he says. "But by and large, I think you do best if you just relax and look at it as a job and go about your work methodically."

I was thinking more along the lines of blind rage. But I figured I'd better defer to the voice of experience—especially when I discovered that his machine has eight hand levers and three foot pedals.

Like most things in life, trashing buildings is more complicated than it first appears. Even if you manage to figure out what all those controls do, you're still not out of the woods.

Swing the boom too far and too fast, for instance, and the world of physics will grab the ball and begin to direct it toward your cab—which, for reasons that should be fairly obvious, is not a good thing.

Webb gave me what amounted to a warm-up exercise—breaking stuff by simply dropping the big ball on top of it. We found a couple of huge pieces of the concrete skin lying on the ground outside what used to be the west entrance. After a mere 10 or 15 minutes of instruction, I figured out how to release the brake on the hoist . . . gun the throttle to raise the ball . . . let the ball go . . . and WHAM!

Massive holes. Life is good.

Webb warned me that my job would get trickier. Momentum, he said, is a powerful thing. Sometimes, he said, the ball seems to control the crane, rather than vice versa.

He moved the giant machine off to the side, where he figured I couldn't get into too much trouble while practicing. Ha! Fooled him! Dr. Destructo accidentally maimed a perfectly good deciduous tree and nearly obliterated an equipment trailer.

Clearly, I was ready.

We drove the ponderous beast to the northeast corner and lined it up between two hefty concrete walls that once guarded the performers' entrance. Between those walls, down a long, wide, concrete ramp, had passed some of the world's finest entertainers and athletes. I remember walking up that ramp one night next to Michael Jordan as he headed to the team bus after knocking the Cavs out of the playoffs for the millionth time.

But Jordan never faced a defense like this.

I whammed on the right wall. I whammed on the left wall. I knocked off a metal sign. I splintered concrete. Dust flew. Rods bent. The relentless, cathartic thud of ball against wall continued for so long that Webb should have signed over part of his paycheck.

This was the next-to-last day in the 25-year life of the Coliseum. All that still stood would come down the following day with simultaneous tugs on two vertical beams. Then the last scraps would be pushed into the big hole in the ground and plowed over. In the end, only a meadow would remain. Not so much as a plaque. Just memories.

As they say, all things must pass. But must they pass this quickly?

A bit misty-eyed, I drove to the exit and spotted a longtime security guard wearing a faded Coliseum uniform top. I looked at him and shook my head.

"A $9 million meadow," he said bitterly, referring to the price paid by the National Park Service.

I told him not to forget the $150 million we paid for Gund Arena.

"You can't fight politics," he snarled, "and you can't fight greed."

Maybe not. But when all else fails, at least you can smash stuff.

June 6, 1999

Middle-Aged Man & the Sea

MIAMI: With all this talk about Marlins, I figured I'd better go catch one.

After all, what kind of responsible journalist would write a series of stories about the Florida Marlins without first conducting a thorough investigation?

Exactly. That's my story for the accounting department and I'm sticking to it.

So I scan the ads and spot a charter boat named *Therapy*. Which is exactly what a Northeast Ohioan needs after watching half the population of Miami walking around in foam Marlin heads.

As the sun rises on the morning of World Series Game 2, I hop onto the 57-foot fishing yacht and prepare to stare into the belly of the baseball-appropriated beast.

The *Therapy* is a serious boat. Big bridge. Big, loud diesel engines. Staffed by a couple of grizzled, oceangoing veterans.

My new best pal—First Mate Rick Masters—is precisely the man I need. On June 8, he nailed the biggest blue marlin caught around Miami since 1983.

"It was 426 pounds on the scale—and his head was still lying on the ground," Masters says as our boat rips toward the horizon, spreading a wake through the Atlantic just north of Miami Beach.

Ah, the romance. Me and Hemingway. Fighting the Big One. Cranking and pulling and straining and dueling, man against beast.

The *Therapy's* customers on this glorious morning are four men who showed up independently, ranging from an 18-year-old Colombian to an 81-year-old from Atlanta.

As we head out into the Gulf Stream, Rick reveals his game plan: First catch a few "flippers," small bonitas that will be used as bait for the bigger fish.

Rick has a deep tan and long, reddish hair that he pulls back into a ponytail, then divides into six braided strands that are finished off with colored beads. In his left ear is a gold earring. Around his neck is a heavy silver necklace with a big sailfish medallion.

A pair of all-purpose fisherperson pliers are poised in a little holster on his right hip.

Completing the look is a pair of big rubber boots, black jeans and a T-shirt reading: "Second place is the first loser."

The Rickster says he has been doing this for 22 years—and he's only 32.

"I grew up in the [Florida] Keys and never wanted to do anything but fish, [scuba] dive and get drunk—and I was too young to get drunk," he says, laughing.

But once he was of age, he drank enough to float a boat.

"I gave up drinking three years ago," he confides halfway through the four-hour journey. "In this business, it's pretty predominant that people drink or take drugs. I have a 7-year-old daughter, and when I drink I'm not around much."

Rick says people like him, working two trips a day for a "good boat," can average $20,000 a year.

In his mind, a "good boat" is one run by an active owner, a guy who drums up steady business by delivering fish to the concierges at area hotels.

If the pay is lame, the view from the office isn't too shabby. As the *Therapy* trolls along, we can see the reflection of the tropical sun on the rolling water . . . lobstermen checking their traps . . . gulls cruising for an easy meal . . . and the skyscrapers of Miami Beach looking like Lego towers in the distance.

"None of those office jobs for me," Rick says. "Breathing that air-conditioning all day? Are you kidding me?"

There are other perks, too: "You get to meet people of every race, creed and religion in the world." Including Marlins.

So just how tough are they? The fish, I mean.

"They're a very beautiful fish, very strong," Rick says. "I saw a marlin eat a 25-pound dolphin in one bite. Unbelievable."

Around Miami, marlin are caught mainly in the summer and weigh 200 to 250 pounds.

"Out of 50 boats, maybe 20 hook a marlin. The food's just not here for them—and they've been overfished."

Obviously, Rick has plenty of time to chat. Lots of time. Lots and lots of time. After two hours, our boat hasn't had a single nibble. All hands are getting a bit restless.

"Bad day," Rick mutters.

How many days does this happen in a year? "Probably 50."

Perfect. A freak drought.

Then, suddenly, activity off the starboard stern.

Eighteen-year-old Andres Botero, visiting the States from Colombia, hops into a chair and goes to work.

He reels and reels and reels some more. About five minutes later, he hauls up a king mackerel, about 3 feet long. Not bad, but not exactly the ultimate catch.

It is the only fish the *Therapy* will get the entire time.

Deep-sea fishing? Ha. This is more like deep-sea boating.

If you ask me, this whole marlin thing is highly overrated. If these fish are so big and bad, why won't they show their pointy little heads?

But perhaps we shouldn't get too worked up about this. After all, the Cleveland Indians appear to be close to bagging their limit.

Oct. 21, 1997

Wilt's Old Car Has Plenty of Legroom

Anyone who followed the career of Wilt Chamberlain knows he is defined by two historic numbers: 100 and 20,000.

The first figure is the number of points he scored in a single game, an NBA record that has stood for 49 years.

The second number is unofficial, but if accurate, might be even more impressive, perhaps dating all the way back to Giacomo Casanova in the 18th century.

According to Wilt's autobiography, 20,000 is the number of women he, um, got to know.

The 7-foot-1, 300-pound superstar distinguished himself in another arena as well.

"He had good taste in cars," says Myron Vernis, general manager of Glenmoor Country Club in Jackson Township, where the 17th annual Glenmoor Gathering of Significant Automobiles rolls into action this weekend.

Wilt was partial to Italian bodies (so to speak). He not only owned Maseratis, as did many other wealthy folks, but also for 30 years he drove an Italian car unlike any other.

His customized, bright red Ghia 450 SS is among a vast array of amazing vehicles that will be on public display at Glenmoor, which annually hosts one of the best car shows in the nation.

The hand-built Ghia 450 SS was sold for just one year, 1966. Only 52 were built—and this was the first.

The car originally was owned by Hollywood producer Burt Sugarman, who essentially created the model.

At an auto show in Geneva in 1964, Sugarman fell in love with a Ghia 230 S. But the manufacturer had no plans to sell those in the United States because they weren't powerful enough for American highways. So Sugarman asked the company to create something similar but with a big V-8 engine.

Ghia agreed, and Sugarman set up a dealership in Beverly Hills. Most of the buyers were friends of his, generally TV and movie stars.

The Glenmoor car was the prototype and Sugarman's personal

car for three years. He sold it to his pal Wilt in 1969, while the Big Dipper was employed by the Los Angeles Lakers.

Now, when somebody measures 85 inches from head to toe, a bit of customization is in order. The big man retained the original black-leather seats, but had them moved *waaaaay* back. How far? Well, with the driver's seat rolled all the way back, a 6-foot-1 man can't even reach the pedals.

Chamberlain also customized the wooden dash, adding gauges that were more contemporary and installing a new stereo, "the best Craig cassette player available in the mid-'70s," Vernis jokes.

Most of all, big Wilt wanted a bigger engine. The original 273 cubic-inch four-barrel was just too wimpy. So he swapped it out for a modified Chevy small-block that pushed the horsepower from 250 to 350.

In 1999, after Chamberlain went off to that big locker room in the sky, Vernis bought the car from his estate at an auction. The fact it had been owned by a basketball icon didn't influence his decision, says Vernis, who is well-known among collectors.

"It was available, and I had always liked these cars."

Vernis got lucky, paying only $23,000. Today, it's worth $110,000 to $125,000. The Wilt connection adds little to the relative value because the 26 still in existence "were pretty much all celebrity-owned," he says.

Among serious collectors, the real magic of this car comes from its status as the prototype.

Vernis doesn't baby his gem. Of the 35,000 miles on the odometer, about 10,000 are his. Recently he drove it to a show in northern Michigan and back, racking up 1,000 miles in one day.

"It's not a great handling car, but it's very, very fast, and a great cruising car."

That's for sure. On Thursday, despite intermittent rain, Vernis tossed me the keys and let me cruise.

The Ghia is indeed fast and fun. And the handling didn't seem bad, either. Of course, I wasn't exactly spoiled—the last time I was at Glenmoor, I drove a 1939 Rolls-Royce Phantom III that handled like an apartment building.

As I was zooming around in Wilt's old car, terrorizing the Glen-moor residents, I was tempted to pull over and look under the seat for a little black book. But then I realized Wilt's book probably wouldn't even fit in the trunk.

Sept. 16, 2011

Panhandler for a Day

I'm not certain whether this is a good thing or a bad thing, but I have discovered that I am a terrible panhandler.

While wearing my official City of Akron Temporary Panhandler Registration badge—Number T-083, for those of you scoring at home—I didn't collect enough money to pay for the gas I burned while driving to three sites.

My dismal showing stands in stark contrast to that of the local pros. Yes, pros. There is so much money to be made that at least one panhandler, a guy who hangs out near the University of Akron, is paid by someone to stand there and collect.

One beggar near the Wallhaven Acme boasted to a donor that he had made $40,000 the previous year.

Yet another, when offered food by a female motorist, replied, "If I take home anymore [bleeping] food, my wife will kill me."

Some beggars wear iPods and sip Starbucks. Just how destitute can they be?

Statistics provided by the Akron police show that 21 percent of the people who have registered under the city's 2-year-old panhandling law don't live in the city.

"For many of the people who get these permits, it is a profitable business," says Dave Lieberth, Akron's deputy mayor of administration and the driving force behind the legislation. "Some of these people are taking the bus in every morning from out of town. This is their job!"

Lieberth says the new law has cut down dramatically on complaints about aggressive panhandling. But it clearly has done nothing to reduce the number of people standing around with their hands out.

No wonder. Forty grand, tax-free?

Hmmm. With my stock portfolio reduced to a rotting carcass, I figured this might be worth a shot.

Could it really be that easy? Only one way to find out.

Now, the concept of a "panhandling license" seems absurd. What self-respecting panhandler would apply for a license?

Incredibly, police say about 99 percent of the people they check have one. So I figured I'd better fall in line.

The first step was a trip to the cop shop, where the permits are issued free of charge.

As Lieberth points out, qualifying is not particularly difficult. "Apparently you did, so that's a pretty clear test that anybody can get one," he said.

Funny.

Actually, Dave, in an eerie foreshadowing, I initially was rejected.

I showed up at police headquarters in the middle of a Wednesday afternoon and was directed to a third-floor office. When I got there, I was told drug-testing was being conducted in that office and they didn't want to "compromise" the area. Try another time, they said.

Three hours later, I returned and was allowed to compromise their area. After coughing up all kinds of personal information, including a Social Security number and date of birth, I smiled for the camera and was given a temporary badge good for 10 days. If I cleared the background check, I could get a "permanent" license good for one year.

Panhandlers also are handed a sheet of paper spelling out the rules—a mere 60 lines of type on one side and 59 on the other—ALL IN CAPITAL LETTERS.

The main restrictions: Stay at least 20 feet away from banks, bus stops, ATMs, sidewalk cafes, schools, churches, Canal Park stadium, the Akron Civic Theatre, Lock 3 Park and the Akron Art Museum.

Being a fair-weather panhandler, I waited for a nice day. That morning, I tore apart a cardboard box and, Magic Marker in hand, vowed to adhere to the rule that says you can't lie about how the money will be used.

I settled on "Please help the Homeless." That was legit because I planned to donate whatever I collected to Access Inc., a local shelter for women and children.

Next, I needed a game plan. I would require not only a high-traffic area but also a place where I could stand on the driver's side of the car. That's easy in England; not so easy here.

A colleague suggested a spot where he had seen other panhandlers: Buchholzer Boulevard and Independence Avenue, immediately west of Chapel Hill Mall. A grassy median and a traffic light supply a captive audience with driver's-side access.

When I arrived, another beggar was already there. The nerve!

His sign, sadly, was more compelling: "Anything will help. Homeless, hungry, need work."

I also realized I might be a bit overdressed, despite wearing blue jeans, a cheap knit shirt, sunglasses and a ballcap. (Note to self: Next time, go with the tattered T-shirt.)

Plan B was the eastern edge of the University of Akron campus. A one-way access road that parallels state Route 8 offers a driver's-side patch of real estate at Carroll and Goodkirk.

The juices began to flow. My panhandling debut!

Almost immediately, I began to regret it.

A distinct sociological pattern quickly emerged. When motorists first lay eyes on you, their faces communicate one of two emotions:

• Pity.
• Contempt.

Being on the receiving end of either one isn't much fun.

After the initial eye contact, a third reaction usually kicks in: avoidance. It is amazing how creative people can be when they want to dodge eye-contact. Suddenly, all sorts of things need to be rearranged on the front seat, in purses or in center consoles.

I stood there for half an hour; it seemed like half a day.

During the entire ordeal, my only donation was a $1 bill, courtesy of a young woman of college age who made the hand-off at about 10 mph.

I attributed my lack of success to my location. College kids are cheap, right?

So it was off to the Wallhaven neighborhood in West Akron, where one lane of eastbound Market Street peels off toward Exchange and Hawkins at a stoplight in front of a muffler shop.

Less than one minute after assuming my position, a middle-age black woman in a rusty car rolled down her window and handed me a crumpled dollar.

Bingo! This must be the spot.

Wrong. Thirty minutes later, my total Wallhaven haul was . . . one dollar.

I did collect some local flavor, though. About midway through, a teenage boy driving in the other direction rolled down his window and screamed, "Get a [bleepin'] job!"

Truth be told, that was a welcome respite from the alternating looks of pity and disdain.

I returned to the office bemoaning the fact that this idea looked a whole lot better on paper.

"Well," offered colleague David Giffels, "if there's an upside, you're just not pathetic enough."

Maybe I should have listened to Managing Editor Doug Oplinger, who suggested I could gain a vast amount of sympathy by wearing a shirt with a Merrill Lynch logo.

In any event, I have passed along my hard-earned $2, plus $23 more, to Access Inc., which for 24 years has aided local homeless women and children.

If you really want to help the homeless, that makes a lot more sense than trying to guess whether someone is truly destitute. Just write a check to Access, the Haven of Rest, the Interfaith Hospitality Network or a similar group.

The city recently created another alternative. Two old parking meters have been painted and turned into donation receptacles. Coins deposited in a special green meter inside of Lock 3 Park go to the Haven of Rest ($100 so far after only a couple of months), and donations dropped into a red meter newly placed at Cascade Plaza will be forwarded to the Salvation Army.

Granted, none of this addresses the problem of homeless people who want to be homeless because they're mentally ill. But that's a tougher topic for another day.

One thing is certain: Throwing bills at people who might or might not desperately need them isn't the best strategy.

Those folks will always be out there, because the courts have consistently ruled that begging is protected by freedom of speech. Akron's law is about as restrictive as possible.

Meanwhile, I've come to the conclusion that panhandling is an overrated profession. Sure, it might sound great when your school guidance counselor recommends it, but you'd better do some job-shadowing before you commit.

Oct. 17, 2008

WEIRD SCENES INSIDE THE GOLD MINE

The Buzzards Return to . . . Clinton?

That scandal in the New York governor's office is nothing compared to this.

We come before you today to blow the lid off the biggest public relations scam since the invention of the media.

Dateline: Hinckley.

The first buzzard of spring? *Puh-leeze.*

The buzzards in that Medina County burg are nothing but no-good procrastinators. You want real buzzard action? Forget the sacred Hinckley ceremony this weekend. Head to Clinton. Right now.

Yes, you heard me right. Clinton. Down near Canal Fulton. Cozy little town just off state Route 21 in dear old Summit County. The real capital of Hurray-It's-Almost-Spring Day.

Clinton's buzzards have already been back for well over a week. My special Clinton operative, Lynn Westfall, reports that the first ugly avatar came flapping in on March 3.

"They're always in Clinton before they hit Hinckley," says Mayor Phyllis Mayberry, who has called Clinton home for 43 years. "We've had as many as 50 nesting down in our trees."

Mayberry and her husband live in Warwick Park, right next to a stand of pines that serves as Buzzard Central. So many buzzards hang around there at times that a couple of trees were destroyed by all the droppings.

"I'd go through there honking my horn and they'd all take off, and as soon as I'd leave, they'd all come back," says Mayberry.

It should come as no surprise that Clinton—Ohio's 550th most populated place—doesn't have much experience in putting together PR juggernauts. The mayor presides over a population of 1,404 (not including winged scavengers) and is the casual, down-to-earth sort.

She'd never dream of trying to drum up a pseudo, Hinckleyesque news event.

So we did it for her.

Exactly one week ago today—March 6, 2008—at precisely 2:35 p.m., Ranger Bob spotted a big ol' turkey vulture swooping just above a tree line on top of a hill.

Ranger Kenny Love, armed with a 600 mm telephoto lens, documented the moment through the magic of pixels.

And the rest shall be history.

Take *that,* Hinckley.

On the other hand . . . towns should be careful what they wish for.

"Oh, they're ugly," admits the mayor. "Uglier than ugly. They have that red beak on them and stuff. People think they're turkeys when they see 'em."

The big raptors also live on the wrong side of the tracks.

Warwick, after which Warwick Park was named, was once a hamlet outside Clinton proper. But Warwick was behaving improperly. The Ohio & Erie Canal, which gave birth to the village, brought an influx of rowdy residents, and that tradition continued long after the canal gave way to the railroad.

In the 1950s, when old Army barracks were dragged in to house the railroaders, Clinton had seen enough, and annexed Warwick to gain some control through zoning.

Hey, maybe Clinton can annex Hinckley.

Although Mayberry appears to be a mellow mayor (we'll skip the obvious joke about her last name), don't get the impression she's a pushover. She recently outlasted the notoriously glacier-paced Federal Emergency Management Agency, duking for 2½ years to nail down funding to relocate six families who suffered severe flood damage.

Those families rose from the swamps to higher ground. And continued to move up, ever higher, way up to the peaks, where they now gaze out over the luscious landscape, soaring with the majestic—nah. We can only take this so far.

March 13, 2008

BMV Dislikes Your Plate? 2BAD4U

They meet every morning in downtown Columbus. Fifteen of them, ranging from clerks to bigwigs. They're as young as 25 and as old as 60.

That diverse collection of folks is charged with coming to a daily consensus—and doing it by 10 a.m.

Meet the Special Plates Review Committee, a group of state employees that decides what you can and can't put on your license plate.

You ask, they decide. And a lot of times, they don't like what you ask.

During the past two years alone, the Ohio Bureau of Motor Vehicles has turned down 1,574 different requests for customized plates.

You know the kind of plates we're talking about. Stuff like SCRMOM or CATLOVR or BUCKSFN instead of the random collection of numbers and letters you get right off the shelf.

The BMV calls them "personalized" plates. The rest of us call them "vanity" plates. By either name, their owners must pony up an extra $35—not just once, but every year the plates are used.

Ohio's tags are required to have at least four, but not more than seven, letters and/or numbers. But that still permits ample opportunity for some amazingly creative stuff.

As you know, creativity can take many forms. If it were up to some Ohio drivers, they would use their license plates to express their loathing for someone or something (IH8MYX) . . . or confess to recreational drug habits (2TOKE) . . . or share with the motoring world their fondness for a particular type of carnal activity (nah— I'd never get that into the paper).

In other words, I defy you to read through the list of banned plates and keep a straight face.

If you want to try, head to our website, where we've posted all 1,574 plates that have been nixed since the end of 2006.

Some of the rejections are no-brainers. The F-word, in all its glorious combinations, variations, permutations and amalgamations, could fill a couple of phone-book pages all by itself.

Similarly, a horde of people wanted to tell us who or what "sucks"—everything from Michigan to SUVs to work to the Florida Gators to the cold. Forget it. The BMV has decreed that nothing shall suck.

Other drivers would sentence people or entire groups to a permanent home in what the Greeks referred to as Hades. Can we all agree that's probably not the best sentiment to express within easy view of youthful eyes?

But some of the rejected combinations seem awfully mild—TUSH, for instance, or DEEPDO or IGOTGAS.

And some of the rejections are incomprehensible. RX4FUN was a no-go. You mean I can't proclaim that my car is my prescription for fun? Or that my classic Mazda RX7 doesn't bring a big smile to my face?

And is there something wrong with being a NEATFRK, other than running the risk of clashing with a sloppy roommate?

The BMV says there's a method to its madness. It says it bars plates that:

• " . . . are profane, obscene, sexually explicit or scatological."

• " . . . could reasonably be expected to provoke a violent response from viewers without additional comment."

• " . . . advocate lawlessness."

Now, does the BMV really believe the plate UEEDIOT would foment physical confrontations in the streets?

Some plates from the Land of the Banned seem inappropriate only in certain contexts. If you're driving a Hummer H2, for instance, who could object to a plate that reads HMMRR?

If the plate belonged to a teenage boy driving a sub-compact beater, well, we're probably looking at a different meaning.

Similarly, on a classic 1946 Ford station wagon, WOODY12 might be a perfectly fine plate. But to the folks in Columbus, apparently, it's a state of arousal.

After a while, the whole thing seems a bit like a Rorschach test. When I looked at "USUK05," my initial thought was "United States, United Kingdom" and the number five. On a different day, I might have seen "you suck" and the number five.

Or how about FBLUOSU? Could be "football—love you OSU." On the other hand, it could also be "f- - - Blue—OSU."

The plate police look at this stuff from every conceivable angle. They check different languages (hence the demise of BITEMOI). They run the combinations through Internet dictionaries of urban slang.

Which is probably wise. In some circles, a "basshead" is not an avid fisherman but a crack fiend.

"Rice" can be used as a derogatory term for a modified Japanese import car. You'll get no rice from the BMV.

Even the once-benign term "tea bag" now has sexual connotations.

The BMV claims it doesn't err on the side of prudism.

"We err on the side of balance between freedom of speech and limiting profanity, offensiveness or phrases that could incite lawlessness," says Lindsey Bohrer, a spokeswoman for the Ohio Department of Public Safety.

Others have accused the bureau of criminal stodginess. In fact, the big review panel is the result of a consent agreement between the BMV and the American Civil Liberties Union.

Based on figures supplied by the BMV, the rejection rate is about 2 percent.

Some rejections don't involve taste. Certain placements of zeros and the letter "O" are forbidden simply because they could create confusion in the law-enforcement community as to which is which.

But most of the turndowns involve the BMV assuming the worst. The panel concluded, for example, that MORHED7 was not a bow to Morehead State University's class of 2007.

And that SHGWAGN had nothing to do with REO Speedwagon and everything to do with a British term for something else.

And that the guy who wanted SUPRBLS was not necessarily a football fan.

Rejected motorists do have an appeal process. They can write directly to the state registrar within 30 days. But if he turns thumbs down, it's ballgame.

The BMV said it could not supply figures on how many rejections are appealed or how many appeals succeed.

But we do know this: There's absolutely no truth to the rumor that Michael Phelps is the driver who is appealing the rejection of LKABONG.

Feb. 13, 2009

'Gay Akron' Needs Some Work

I arrived in Akron in 1984. Since then, I have witnessed approximately 729,124 schemes to turn this city into a tourist destination.

These days, news of another new proposal usually triggers either a weary sigh or a hearty chuckle. The latest drew both.

That would be the plan to transform Akron into a hot spot for gays.

Now, you shouldn't need an M.B.A. from Wharton to realize that's just not going to happen.

Let's say you're a gay guy sitting in your tastefully decorated apartment in Des Moines. You're bored, and you start to fantasize about a vacation.

Your initial thoughts may drift toward Provincetown, Mass., a beachfront community known far and wide for its gay friendliness. That place is so gay-friendly that it can be ungay-unfriendly.

Or perhaps our daydreamer is more the West Coast type, in which case San Francisco looms large. The City by the Bay first had an openly gay city supervisor way back in the 1970s. No American big city is gay-friendlier.

Little Key West would undoubtedly work, too.

But I will bet you a year's supply of rainbow stickers that our gay guy in Iowa will never start daydreaming about Akron, Ohio. Not now, not ever. We could spend $50 million on brochures and websites and networking plans, and it still ain't gonna happen.

That rather obvious reality came crashing down quickly on the latest brainstorm, a bid by the Akron/Summit County Convention & Visitors Bureau to identify and market gay-friendly businesses to prospective tourists.

The CVB wanted to meet last week with local business folks who believed they had something special to offer America's gays. The response was so meager that the meeting was canceled.

When you have trouble selling a product—e.g., Gay Akron— the problem is not always the sales staff. You can't sell what you don't have. And Akron simply doesn't have much to offer to the gay market that the gay market can't find in a hundred other cities across the continental United States.

If you don't think this latest scheme is laughable, just randomly ring up somebody in Provincetown.

Rick Reynolds, assistant general manager of the Crown and Anchor Inn, which bills itself online as gay-owned and -operated, was laughing so hard that he nearly dropped the phone when told of Akron's scheme.

"I'm heading there tomorrow," he joked.

If he does, that will mark his Akron debut. "Isn't there some tires there or something?"

Apparently, Reynolds doesn't realize that we have become incredibly cool since adding bike racks to the front of our city buses.

While we keep trying to tell people we're cool, Provincetown is telling its *visitors* how to be cool.

And, as it turns out, our 10-digit phone numbers are a full six degrees of separation from cool. A gay Provincetown website advises visitors: "Be cool. When you give out your number, just use the last four digits. . . . Every phone number in P'town starts with the same area code and exchange—508-487."

Akron's latest marketing thud has nothing to do with sexual orientation. We are not suddenly going to become a magnet for straight people, either. Or big people or small people.

Twinsburg seems to have connected with double people, but that's an aberration.

Sure, we should keep trying to pump up our convention business, and we can attract some outsiders with an inventors' hall or a revamped art museum or a marathon or this week's big golf tournament. Those things are well worth pursuing, not only for their regional drawing power but also to give the locals a better quality of life.

Let's get this straight, though: Nobody is going to travel hundreds of miles to vacation in Akron unless family or friends live here.

And that's OK. Did anybody ever move to Akron thinking that some day it would become the Orlando of the Midwest?

July 31, 2007

Million-Dollar Pal

At first, I thought she was kidding. At second, I thought she was kidding. Finally, she convinced me she was serious: Would I agree to serve as a "lifeline" for her brother, who was about to make an appearance on *Who Wants To Be a Millionaire?*

Egads.

What a complex person her brother must be—smart enough to qualify as a contestant, dumb enough to want my help.

Still, he wanted me. And, like most people, I need to feel wanted.

Yes, I will be his lifeline. I will throw a rope to this poor, misguided lad of 39, this Greg Snelson, this 1979 graduate of Revere High, this owner of an MBA from Carnegie Mellon who works as a computer wizard in Charlotte, N.C. I will steady him, fill in his mental blanks and hold him close as we shoot into the hot glare of the national spotlight, returning home with one million buckaroonies.

The sister, Kathy Pietz, a neighbor and friend, soon hooked us up for a get-acquainted phone call. During our chat, he asked about my areas of expertise. I told him I had none. He laughed. Apparently, he thought I was joking.

The rest of Snelson's lifeline lineup was impressive: a physician, a professor, a minister and a pal who is a walking encyclopedia of movies and music. Obviously, that left him in desperate need of a person who writes goofy stuff for a newspaper.

Snelson is nothing if not persistent. Over the last year, he and his wife called the show's 800 number about 75 times. About 25 times he passed the first round of three questions, but couldn't survive the second round of five. Finally, in mid-August, he made his breakthrough.

The show was taped Sept. 14 and is scheduled to air tonight at 9 on WEWS (Channel 5).

I was told that, on the morning of the taping, ABC would call me between 9 a.m. and noon and outline the ground rules. With only 10 minutes left on the clock, a pleasant soul named Gina rang to tell me that, if Greg made it into the "hot seat" that evening, a producer would call to alert me. The next call would be Regis.

I was to let the phone ring three times, then pick up and simply say, "Hello." No speakerphones. No TV or radio in the background.

The call would come between 5 and 8 p.m.— meaning my volunteer work could keep me glued to the phone for a total of six hours. The good news: I wouldn't be alone. Lifelines are allowed to recruit their own lifelines.

The house began to fill up shortly before 5. The experts-in-waiting included Greg's parents, Al and Neva; his sister; my wife; and several other Mensa candidates of various ages. We quickly assembled our game plan: I would repeat the question and the choices, and my helpers would scrawl their choices on a piece of paper, along with their percentage of certainty.

As the clock struck 5, we ate appetizers. As the clock struck 6, we ate pizza. As the clock struck 7, we turned on the Indians game.

A watched phone never rings.

Suddenly, at 7:23 p.m., a jingle. I jumped. His parents absolutely levitated.

Unfortunately, the caller was not a producer but Greg himself, informing us he had come oh-so-close to the hot seat. He had been one of only two contestants to correctly put four TV characters in chronological order, but the other contestant was faster. On his second try, he answered incorrectly. The third time, he was right— but again too slow. The million dollars had drifted from view, setting behind the skyscrapers of Manhattan.

"It's like finishing fourth in the Olympics," he said a couple of days later, still wounded.

So if you tune in tonight to see Greg, look fast. He doesn't get much face time. But at least he got there. He earned a three-day visit to New York, a meal allowance and a bunch of limo rides.

And we, dear readers, have solved a mystery. We now know why *Millionaire* gets such great ratings: If each of the 10 contestants has five lifelines, and each of the five lifelines invites 10 people to the house . . . well, in another month, every person in America will have had a firsthand experience with the show.

You're a sly dog, Regis.

Oct. 1, 2000

Urine Counters Go With the Flow

I'm not quite sure how to introduce this matter in a family news-paper, so maybe I'll just wade right in.

Seems the Ohio Department of Natural Resources commissioned a study that concluded, among other things, that "972,372 bottles of urine are dumped on Ohio's roadsides each year." Now, in my mind, this raises a few questions.

First off: Can we really say with certainty that the total is 972,372 bottles, rather than, say, 972,371 bottles?

Do you know how long it takes to count 972,372 of anything?

Do we have an entire division of state employees who do nothing but count bottles of urine?

Do the people who count the bottles of urine tell their friends what they do for a living?

Can a person punch numbers into a calculator while wearing rubber gloves?

Are most of these bottles wide-mouth, or do Ohioans have incredibly good aim?

Do you get the same score for filling a 7-ounce bottle of Little Kings Cream Ale as you do for filling an empty quart of Bud?

Will future generations of kids ride along in camp buses singing, "972,372 bottles of urine on the wall, 972,372 bottles of urine, take one down, pass it around, 972,371 bottles of urine on the wall. . . ."?

What do the urine counters do with the urine after it has been counted?

How can the urine counters tell the difference between a bottle of urine and an unfinished Mountain Dew?

Before the bottles are counted, must they be stored in an evidence room so they don't end up on the black market as substitute specimens for drug tests?

Does that evidence room have a state-of-the-art ventilation system?

Should the evidence room contain a pool to submerge the vessels that carried the spent fuel, like nuclear power plants?

Should we be laying off some of these urine-counters and using the money to build a LOT more rest stops?

Is Beacon Journal legend Fran Murphey spinning in her grave? (I might be if I had a rest stop named after me, as she does. Hers is on the east side of Interstate 77 near I-271.)

Would more people use rest stops if we named them after movie stars?

If you had a rest stop named after you, would you view it as a compliment?

Could we attract more rest-stop business if we drew targets inside the urinals and awarded lottery-ticket vouchers for the highest scores?

Should we decriminalize indecent exposure in hopes that it would lead to more motorists leaving their urine by the side of the road without leaving all these stinkin' bottles?

If Ohio were one of the states with a bottle deposit, could we fund an entire sewage treatment plant simply by returning all 972,372 bottles?

I didn't want to dip too far into this issue—*eeewww*—but I did ask a couple of other questions that may help clarify the potentially sticky situation.

No, the state doesn't use your tax dollars to pay state employees to count urine. The state uses your tax dollars to outsource the urine counting.

You may be proud to learn that a local company, Davey Resources Group of Kent, was commissioned for this $100,000 study of road-side litter.

Researchers also found answers to questions we didn't even want to ask. In other words, yes, they counted feces containers, too. Those tended to be plastic bags, rather than bottles.

There's a Hefty Bag joke here somewhere, but I'm not gonna touch it.

So what's the point of all this?

Hey, who needs a point when you're using tax money?

Actually, ODNR says, this study will provide a baseline to show whether future anti-littering measures are effective.

In other words, unlike many of us, urine counters have great job security.

I'd propose a toast to them, but that would probably be in bad taste.

July 16, 2004

'Science' Center is Anything But

So you think there's no religion in the public schools? Think again.

For nearly four years, school groups of all types have been rolling up to the Akron Fossils & Science Center in Copley Township, a place that—despite its name—is based squarely on the teachings of the Bible.

It's a small, one-story building at the corner of Cleveland-Massillon and Minor roads, a couple of miles south of Copley Circle. If you go inside and look around, you will discover a paean to creationism.

The "science" being taught includes a huge display quoting the *Book of Genesis* and purporting to show that scientific research confirms every word of the Scripture.

Impressionable youngsters are being taught that the Earth is only 6,000 years old, rather than the 4.5 billion years estimated by the world's scientists. Humans and dinosaurs walked the planet at the same time, according to the displays.

School groups—mostly private but sometimes public—account for the bulk of the center's revenue. That is at best ironic, because every exhibit in the building attempts to shoot down the science of evolution.

Naturally, the center is not a big hit with science teachers. Stephen Weeks, an evolutionary biologist at the University of Akron, thinks the whole operation is "deplorable."

Weeks is among the scholars who have devoted their lives to learning about and teaching the progression of the human race, using the same scientific methods that have brought us this far in physics, chemistry and every other scientific discipline.

I thought it would be great fun to invite Weeks to join me on a tour. It was. But in the end, it was also disheartening.

Weeks had toured the museum before, shortly after it opened. At the time, he wasn't worried because he figured the presentation was so obviously bogus that the operation would never last.

He believes it has survived largely because the center's name misrepresents its mission.

Fudging the name has indeed been effective. The group even fooled the administration at COSI, the renowned science center in Columbus.

COSI was among dozens of mainstream groups that contributed to a fundraising auction for the Copley museum that was held last fall at Copley High School.

COSI spokeswoman Kelli Nowinsky confirmed that her group donated three admission tickets. She said COSI gets "hundreds and hundreds" of requests each year from various organizations and that multiple employees fill the requests.

"Honestly," she says, "the person probably just saw the request and figured they were part of our network" of science museums.

Nowinsky says the folks at COSI "respect all points of view, but not all points of view represent science. We try to present stuff with evidence-based science—if you will, of fact. Respecting the values of others does not mean giving those values equal time."

The Akron Zoo was oblivious, too.

"Their letter for their auction was put into our drawing we hold every month for area nonprofits that do fundraising events," says marketing director David Barnhardt.

He says the zoo is not familiar with the Copley center. "Perhaps we need to gather more information about the organization."

The Cleveland Orchestra says it contributed based solely on the group's name and its status as a nonprofit 501(c)(3) operation.

Perhaps opting for political correctness, COSI, the zoo and the orchestra all declined to say whether they would have withheld support had they known the Copley museum's true nature.

To stage the fundraiser, the center paid $600 to Copley High School for daylong use of the indoor commons. Assistant Superintendent Brian Poe says the school has rented its facilities to other religious groups, so it had no compelling reason to turn these folks away.

Holding a religious meeting at a public school is not nearly as problematic as the fact that Copley-Fairlawn Middle School students made school-sponsored visits to the center before the powers that be figured out the place's actual mission.

But, Poe says flatly, as of last year, "we do not take field trips to the Akron Fossils & Science Center."

Other secular organizations have patronized the place, too, including recreation groups from the city of Ravenna.

The center, which also offers a dinosaur-themed playground called Truassic Park, says it hosts about 3,000 customers a year.

Even when public schools are not sponsoring trips, Weeks says, free tickets are finding their way into children's book bags. Someone (he suspects mothers of other students) stuck tickets in his younger daughter's book bag at preschool and in his older daughter's belongings at her public elementary school.

At parochial schools, of course, religion is an integral part of the curriculum. But the state of Ohio requires parochial schools to meet exactly the same academic standards as other schools.

And, according to the Ohio Board of Education's Academic Content Standards, absorbing the kind of things the Akron Fossils & Science Center is teaching could cause a student to flunk the science portion of his high school graduation test.

For instance, the state says that, by 11th grade, a student should be able to "explain the formation of the sun, Earth and the rest of the solar system from a nebular cloud of dust and gas approximately 4.5 billion years ago."

As early as grade 10, a student should know that "during most of the history of Earth, only single-celled microorganisms existed, but once cells with nuclei developed about a billion years ago, increasingly complex multicellular organisms evolved."

Now, the folks who run the Akron Fossils & Science Center are welcome to believe anything they want. But if they truly believe what they espouse, why not call the place "the Akron Creation Museum" or "the Akron Intelligent Design Center"?

Josiah Detwiler, the center's operations director, says there's no need for that because his group deserves equal time.

"When you go to the Natural History Museum, it doesn't say, 'The Natural History Museum of Evolution,' " he says. "Of course, they're presenting the evolution model of origins there. And so we're making a statement here that, you know, we are presenting science."

He claims evolution is a faith-based approach as well, "because there are unexplainable aspects to it. . . . We're equally as legitimate of an explanation, and that's why we focus the first half of the museum on the science, because the science backs up a supernatural creation."

That assertion draws guffaws from Weeks, the UA professor who joined me for a self-guided tour (at $8 a pop, or $6 each for school groups).

Weeks notes that one of the museum's first displays is labeled "the Failure of Radiometric Dating." Sorry, but if you're taking your Ohio Graduation Tests, you'll need to know that radiometric dating is a proven method of determining geological age by comparing the amount of radioactive isotopes present when a rock was formed to the amount that remains.

The process works because radioactive elements decay at a constant and measurable rate.

In Weeks' view, the alleged "science" at the museum is "so obviously ill-informed that it's just like somebody sat down and said, 'Well, I'm going to come up with a reason why there's no gravity, and just think of stuff off the top of my head.'

"It's arm-waving. It throws out the whole scientific process."

Many of the displays conclude that the assertions of scientists just don't make sense, and that human life is too complex to have simply evolved.

But, as Weeks notes, when earlier humans saw the sun move across the sky, they came to the "logical" conclusion that the Earth was the center of the universe. How could it not be, with the sun rotating around us?

Just because something seems logical doesn't mean it's true.

"We learn things that are counter to what we initially thought," Weeks says. "I think we are learning God's mechanism."

As Weeks points out, evolution and religion are not mutually exclusive.

"I think the processes we use to understand reality are something He instilled in us that really differentiates us from everything else. We've been using those processes extremely well to make what we've made. And we're using those exact same processes to figure out evolution."

If you ask the people at the Akron Fossils & Science Center, though, academia has it all wrong.

"Call the Science Center today to schedule a science class," reads one brochure. "Our teachers are eager to help your student learn more about the beauty and order of creation!"

Most of us spend a lifetime trying to bring order to things that aren't orderly. But that doesn't mean we can.

Feb. 21, 2009

Camping is for Losers

By the time Labor Day rolls around, thousands of folks in our five-county area will have spent all or part of their summer vacation camping.

Which brings to mind one question: What the hell is *wrong* with you people?

Human beings required millions of years to crawl out of the swamps and walk erect. Why reverse the process?

When you go on vacation—those all-too-brief escapades we pine for all year—the idea is not to reduce your standard of living. The guiding principal should be raising your comfort level, stepping up to a glorious existence you normally can't have.

My idea of "roughing It" Is a two-star Holiday Inn. And I won't even do that unless I'm feeling particularly adventurous.

I don't require (nor can I afford) a Ritz-Carlton in every port. But I certainly have no intention of gathering enough on-the-ground experience to engage in a prolonged conversation with an entomologist.

Sleep on the ground? Sure. And after that let's go down and hang out at the bus station.

Why do you think God invented box springs?

Now, don't get me wrong. I think nature is cool. I love to jog through it or bike through it or swim in it. But why give mosquitoes and bees and horseflies a stationary target for hours at a time?

This philosophy tends to irk the woman with whom I have shared a box spring or two.

"How can you rail about cell-phone towers ruining the landscape and then refuse to get out into nature?" inquires my wifely unit.

Bugs.

"You have to put up with a few bugs to see what nature has provided."

I can see nature just fine through a big, clean picture window.

"Camping is an adventure."

So is driving on the Akron Expressway.

"Hrrrumphh."

Hey, I've given this concept a fair shot. I hardly complained at all a few years ago when you asked my dad for a tent for your birthday. My own father! Contributing to your evolutionary delinquency!

"Well, you haven't exactly worn that tent out, have you?"

OK, so you and the kids have used it a little more than I have. A lot more. But what about that night I slept out in the backyard?

"No, you didn't!" pipes up a daughter. "You carried us in because you were cold!"

Whatever.

Look: I realize I'm supposed to love camping. Any red-blooded American is supposed to love camping.

Why do you think Bill "Nature Boy" Clinton used to take those camping-and-hiking vacations out West?

Clinton—the most transparent man in America—wanted to make voters think he was close to the people. Wanted 'em to think that he, too, loves walking through poison ivy in the middle of the night looking for a latrine and some soggy tissue.

But now that Clinton has maxed out on elections, where does he head for his summer vacation? You betcha. Martha's Vineyard—where you need a note from your broker just to get within a mile of the beach.

No tents. No sleeping bags. No downward mobility.

Did Sir James Goldsmith ever risk a case of Lyme disease while trying to unzip some smelly, sweltering, synthetic torture chamber? He did not.

Jimmy used to retreat to his 16,000-acre estate on the Pacific Coast of Mexico, where he had his own hospital, a private town for his help and haciendas for his guests.

Why? Because he could.

Although Jimmy never invited me to Cuixmala before he kicked off, I can guarantee you there wasn't a single portable toilet on the entire 16,000 acres.

So go ahead and brush your teeth with water out of a canteen. Go ahead and cook breakfast on some rusty old pan.

Me? I'm going to order something with an umbrella in it.

Aug. 1, 1997

Up Close & Personal With Angie Everhart

I don't need to explain this format to anybody who reads Playboy, because everybody who reads Playboy reads it for the articles, and the articles always include the Playboy Interview.

That feature is one of the longest-standing traditions in magazine publishing. So the only logical thing to do for a column about this month's cover girl—Akron's Angie Everhart—is turn it into a Q-and-A.

If we follow the Playboy format, first we've gotta give you a bunch of boring biographical stuff, which they always print in italics. Most of us skip right over that part and go to the Q-and-A. Feel free to do that now, because if you know who Angie is, you already know she went to Firestone High, class of '87, where she didn't make the cheerleading squad as a senior and went to the games in a big chicken costume, and then she turned into a world-famous 5-foot-10 supermodel who did things like Sports Illustrated *swimsuit issues, and then she went on Leno and Letterman, and then she got engaged to Sylvester Stallone, and then she got married to George Hamilton's son, Ashley, and then she got divorced, and then she reached the pinnacle of her career when she was interviewed by Stan Piatt on WNIR (100.1-FM) and now, at the creepy old age of 30, she has quit modeling for acting and getting naked.*

But right near the end of the italic part, the magazine always describes the setting for the interview. So I'll tell you that Ms. Everhart and I spent several meaningful minutes together in her palatial suite on the 14th floor of the Ritz-Carlton in Cleveland, where she greeted me, half-dressed, with a big, sloppy kiss. OK, maybe it wasn't exactly that way. Maybe she was wearing a black sweater and slacks and flashed me a thin, forced smile.

ABJ: I heard you flirting with Howard Stern on the radio last week. Does this mean it's over between you and Stan Piatt?

Everhart: Oh, poor Stan. I called him today, but unfortunately, he was already off the air.

ABJ: The way I've heard the story, you begged Piatt to run away with you years ago, but he refused. He said he still had important work to do in Akron and that, as a matter of fact, he really didn't care for redheads. You were devastated. Is that accurate?

Everhart: Yeah. Exactly. Poor Stan. He's always been really sweet to me on the air. I don't know exactly the first time I was on his show. I just remember my brother telling me, "There are these people who talk about you, Angie. We should call." That was the beginning of it.

ABJ: Have you actually gone on a date with Howard Stern?

Everhart: Not yet. Hopefully, I will. He's a lotta fun. He's really smart and actually very nice.

ABJ: Tell your father to quit picking on me. Just because I ridiculed the fancy new "Taj Mahal" plazas on the Ohio Turnpike, he didn't have to write a nasty letter to the editor.

Everhart: Oooooh! You know what? I know who you are! I remember him writing that letter! [Big laugh.]

ABJ: He spent 20 years with ODOT and now he's a consultant, right?

Everhart: He's retired now and works on selected things here in Ohio. He's the smartest guy I know. And I'm not any bit biased.

ABJ: What's the biggest single project he ever worked on?

Everhart: The Ohio Turnpike! My dad had more to do with the Ohio Turnpike than any other engineer in the area!

ABJ: No wonder he's so touchy. But, hey, at least I never got naked in a national magazine.

Everhart: My parents are proud of me. They have their likes and dislikes. There's one photo in Playboy they don't like. I'm sure they could do without the shower picture. Because I am their little girl. They're Mom and Dad. And they're absolutely allowed to have their opinions, and I respect their opinions, and we talk about it. So it's OK.

ABJ: Did you know there's some sort of creature crawling around on your lower back in those pictures?

Everhart: It's not a creature. It's an angel. She has a sword. She's my guardian angel. She's got my back.

ABJ: There's another tattoo on your leg. Did you get them done at the same time?

Everhart: No. They're all different. Different periods of my life. There's a dagger on one side and shamrock on the other.

ABJ: I've got one word for you: Cher.

Everhart: Cher?

ABJ: She was trying to get hers removed, right? Don't you think that somewhere down the line, you might decide this wasn't such a great idea?

Everhart: No. I don't have that many. I have three tattoos, and they're in places where you don't see them—unless I show them to you. They're part of who I am. They're not part of a design. My tattoos all mean something to me. Who knows? Maybe when I'm 80, I'll hate them and want them lasered off. But I'll probably want a lot of things lasered off when I'm 80. [Laughs.]

ABJ: One of the huge news stories in Akron last year involved [Playmate of the Year] Heather Kozar, another naked lady from Akron. They were gonna have her throw out the first pitch at an Aeros game, but their phone lines melted down and they canceled it. Does that kind of commotion surprise you?

Everhart: There's always going to be some kind of controversy over Playboy. There's always going to be somebody who doesn't like what I'm doing or what Heather Kozar is doing or what Howard Stern is doing or what Hugh Hefner is doing or what President Clinton is doing or anybody on the planet—something you're doing.

ABJ: Like your dad.

Everhart: People make choices in their life. I didn't know about Heather!

ABJ: They got 100 phone calls from angry fans.

Everhart: I'm proud of the Playboy pictures. I'm proud to have my face on the cover. I think it's beautiful. I think the pictures are nice. I think they're tasteful. I still left something up to the imagination. If somebody would cancel a job of mine just because of pictures I had done in my career—there's a lot worse things I could do, and it's their loss. Just because she did that, it doesn't make her a bad person at all. I think that's a problem with what America is all about. They're afraid of nudity, but yet they'll put blood and guts on television shows where people are getting killed all over the place. What's wrong with everybody? We were born naked. If she looks good, she can show it. It's her prerogative. And mine.

ABJ: Amen. But you didn't always think that way. I quote from the Akron Beacon Journal of Jan. 20, 1993, when you told Jewell Cardwell: "I will never do a nude. I promised my grandmother that I wouldn't."

Everhart: That just shows you never say never. You know, if you had asked me even a year ago, I probably would have said no. It definitely was a frame of mind for me. I called my grandmother before I did it. She's one of those people who would have called in and said, "I don't want her throwing the baseball." [Laughs.] She might have been one of those 100.

ABJ: Do you have veto power over what pictures they use?

Everhart: Definitely. I had to have control.

ABJ: If you're a superstar, you can get away with that, eh? By the way, what's the difference between a supermodel and a plain ol' regular model?

Everhart: The paycheck.

ABJ: What gets you to the point where you can make $10,000 a day?

Everhart: A lot of work. A lot of determination. Something special about you. A lot of luck. Drive. There's a lot of pretty girls out there who don't make it to the top. You have to be in the right place at the right time. I was lucky. I had something different—I'm a redhead. I got to kind of slide in without any competition.

ABJ: OK, one last question. Is it going to be Stan Piatt or Howard Stern? Make up your mind!

Everhart: I'll go Howard. [Big laugh.]

ABJ: Stan will be crushed. Can I tell him you still love him?

Everhart: Yeah, of course. That would be like dating my brother or something, you know? That would be awful. When you've known somebody so long, it's a whole different thing.

ABJ: Well, gotta go. There's a lot more supermodels waiting for me. *Ciao.*

Jan. 23, 2000

Akron's Bug Crawls to Youngstown

Although the concept of sending a cockroach to Youngstown lends itself to an easy cheap shot, I shall refrain.

In fact, in this case—and this case only—losing a cockroach to Youngstown qualifies as a sad development.

This, my friends, was no ordinary cockroach.

He was a genetic mutation, a 10-foot beast made of brown metal.

With menacing silver eyes.

And long, creepy feelers.

And grotesque arms and legs.

He won a permanent place in Akron lore the instant he mounted that wall at TNT Exterminating on North Main Street, right across from Luigi's

His reign of terror lasted 15 years. But now he has been reduced to living in Youngstown under an assumed name.

Physically, there's nothing wrong with him. To the contrary. He has defied the blazing summers and frigid winters and everything in between.

And he didn't call a news conference to announce he was taking his talents to the South Bank of the Mahoning River.

So what happened?

The gigantic insect was a victim of his own success. The company that commissioned him grew so large it needed a much bigger building.

Owner Michael Grace couldn't find a suitable location for the right price in Akron, so he moved his operation to Macedonia, where he has tripled his square footage and enjoys easy freeway access.

If Grace moved to Macedonia, why did his big bug move to Youngstown? Because Macedonia has absolutely no sense of humor.

Macedonia must think it has turned into Hudson. The city flatly refused to allow the quirky sculpture to besmirch its pristine environs.

"One planning commission guy said, 'Oh, that thing's a landmark. There's no problem,' " Grace says. "The mayor said, 'Nope.' "

Macedonia's loss.

We're talking about an endearing piece of art created by noted Akron sculptor John Comunale—same guy who has been creating high-profile public art for decades.

Comunale's string of Akron hits includes the stainless steel catfish at Furnace and Howard streets, the clock on the Everett Building, Zippy at the McDonald's restaurant near the university and the First Night sculpture at Lock 3 Park.

When he is informed Macedonia exterminated his bug, Comunale replies, "They're a little too touchy up there."

Indeed.

It's also obvious Grace didn't learn the lesson Comunale tried to teach him 15 years ago, when the duo slapped their bug on the wall without mentioning their plans to anyone in power.

"I told Michael it's a lot easier to get forgiveness than permission," jokes the sculptor.

Fortunately, Grace's brother is also in the cockroach biz. So our mighty bug has settled in at Grace Services on Meridian Road, just off Interstate 680. At night, dark-blue lights trained on him from below make him look even more menacing. (The bug, not Grace's brother.)

Grace says his bro encountered absolutely no resistance from Youngstown government.

"If you're a taxpayer there," he notes with a laugh, "they're just happy you're in business."

As the third generation of his family to make a living by maiming Akron's bugs, Grace did not exit our fair city cavalierly.

"We looked all around," he says. "You don't leave Akron after 75 years [without good reason].

"First, I had to be able to afford it. Second, it had to be somewhere that had good freeway access.

"There were [decent] places, but if you're [a long way] from the freeway, that defeats the purpose for us because everything we do we go somewhere."

Grace's 15 employees wage insect wars not only in Cleveland and Akron but as far away as Vermilion and Wooster.

Meanwhile, Comunale, whose Comunale Sculptural Creations

operates out of Canal Place, is on to other things, notably a set of gates for a garden at First Congregational Church on the edge of the University of Akron campus.

In yet another noteworthy development, the cockroach's former home on North Main has been taken over by the Akron Symphony.

Am I the only one picturing a 20-foot violin with a telephone pole for the bow?

June 10, 2012

Area Teens Incriminate Themselves

Hundreds of local schoolkids apparently weren't paying attention when their teachers were talking about the Fifth Amendment.

That would be the one about self-incrimination.

Why else would so many area teens post their photos on the Internet—and sometimes their full names—alongside evidence of illegal activity and/or incredible vulgarity?

No local school system is immune, public or private.

How do we know this? Because these freewheeling kids routinely identify their schools.

And their friends.

And their families.

And their activities.

In fact, they supply enough personal information that any perv on the planet could locate them in five minutes.

If you're a parent who has never prowled around on MySpace (www.myspace.com), you're in for a shock.

In addition to countless photos of underage kids swilling beer and booze, you can find an endless parade of fresh faces dropping enough F-bombs to flatten a small nation.

By clicking on "search" on the top of the MySpace home page, you can sort out people not only by their school but their year of graduation.

Let's hop on my surfboard and take a little cruise.

Why, here's a girl from Archbishop Hoban. She is posing in a black slip. In her right hand is a hand-lettered sign that reads, "I'm not your baby girl." Her left hand is raised, and her middle finger is extended. On the very same page, she is posed, demurely, on a football field in a cheerleading outfit.

Here's a girl from Green High School, listing her general interests: "dancing, camping, fishing, science, spiritual things, getting f- - - - - up."

(The dashes are not hers; they're ours. That's the case throughout this report.)

Here are two more girls from Green, faces clearly identifiable.

They're in a bedroom. One is lying on the bed, wearing fishnet stockings with large tears. The other is between her legs, apparently trying to rip off the rest of the stockings.

A girl from Cuyahoga Falls, staring directly at the camera, poses in a short skirt, hiked up on one side, next to the words, "You know you want this." Her "general interests" include "GUYS, partys [sic], the mall, shopping, driving, SEX!!!" She also informs us that she's "not scared to try anything new!!"

A fellow who identifies himself as a member of the Cuyahoga Falls High School band says he has taken "a lot" of drugs but "haven't overdosed yet. Yeah!"

Here are three cute girls from Revere, each wearing a T-shirt with a different hand-drawn letter. They are lined up in this order: H-O-E.

A Copley boy shares with the world his first thoughts upon rising each morning: "F- - - F- - - S- - - F- - -." Thanks for sharing.

A Jackson High boy says his general interests including "hanging out with my friends and drinking." In case we need proof, he supplies a photo of himself, eyes closed, with the caption: "I'm passed out drunk." You don't need to be part of a CSI team to figure out his identity: His page features a photograph of his school ID with his full name clearly visible.

One Wadsworth girl doesn't sound particularly approachable. Her headline reads, "I punch b- - - - - - in the f- - - - - - face." Pleased to meet you, dear.

Wadsworth also boasts the unofficial winner in the self-incrimination category, a carefree dude whose general interests are "sports, weightlifting, cars, Coors Light and Killian's Irish red."

In one photo, he is downing a shot. In another, he poses with an upraised glass of beer, staring right at the camera. In yet another photo, he is holding a different glass of beer at a New Year's Eve party. A fourth incriminating photo shows him with a pal, beer in hand, above the caption, "Drinking at the beach house."

A chap from Stow High created this headline: "Bend over, b- - - -! It's time for a spanking."

A Tallmadge boy says, "I love to smoke. I do it on a daily basis. That's the ganja, man."

At Highland, we are treated to multiple photos of a girl partying in a room at a Holiday Inn. In one shot, she and a girlfriend are dancing wildly, beer in hand, while a boy sits in the corner next to a beer on a nightstand.

On another Highland site, a young man answers, "F- - - yeah" three times when asked whether he has drunk alcohol, smoked or done drugs.

Elsewhere, he weighs in on the joys of reading. "I don't read unless I am reading in class. F- - - books!!!!!"

This parade continues, on and on, through such disparate schools as Garfield, Walsh Jesuit, Norton, Lake, Coventry, Hudson, Barberton, St. Vincent-St. Mary, Springfield, Western Reserve Academy, North, Cloverleaf, Manchester, Highland, Ellet, Woodridge and Kenmore.

But just when you start to get thoroughly depressed by the level of discourse, you are treated to some comic relief.

Here's a Norton girl talking about her fantasy flame: "I wanna meet Troy #8 who was on the Dallas Cowboys. Even though he is like 40-something, I would marry him anyways." Mr. Aikman would undoubtedly be thrilled to know that his potential bride not only considers him elderly but can't remember his last name.

How about this one, from a boy who attends Cuyahoga Falls High? In filling out the section for his favorite movies, he writes: "I really don't like any new movies, but the old classics, like Super Troopers [and] Remember the Titans."

Now there's a student with historical perspective. Casablanca . . . Citizen Kane . . . and . . . Super Troopers.

By the time you read this, many of these pages might have been yanked by their owners, or at least set to "private." (When a MySpacer sets his or her profile to private, only people he or she preapproves can view the material.) But even when a site is set to private, that same person can wind up being outed on someone else's site, thanks to group photos or another user posting comments from friends.

One wonders whether coaches, band directors and principals have spent any time surfing MySpace, given the fact that most schools require students participating in athletics and other extracurricular activities to sign a pledge promising not to drink or smoke.

One also wonders how many parents know what kind of face their offspring are presenting to the entire wired universe.

Most of all, one wonders why all of these young people fail to realize that the Internet is as public as public can be.

We'll try to gather some feedback and pass it along.

Jan. 25, 2007

Area Teens See the Light

Regular users of MySpace may have noticed numerous changes during the last five days.

Many of the Web pages maintained by local high school students have been altered, taken down or set to "private" in the wake of our report showing that hundreds of local teens were posting self-incriminating photos and comments.

Personal sites rife with vulgarity and alcohol and drug references have not disappeared—not by a long shot—but plenty of teens seem to have gotten the message that there's a good reason this thing is called the World Wide Web.

All of their scrambling would seem to contradict the dismissive assertion by half a dozen young e-mailers that writing anything about MySpace was "old news."

Teachers and administrators certainly didn't consider it stale.

Many teachers used the column for classroom discussions. At least one private school, Walsh Jesuit, immediately mailed a letter to parents, warning that students whose postings violate school rules "will be disciplined accordingly, and a consequence certainly could include asking the student to leave the school."

Reaction to last week's column—literally hundreds of calls, e-mails and Web postings—was fascinating.

Until 2:30 p.m. on the day of publication, about 95 percent of the feedback was positive. Parents and educators praised the newspaper for shining a light on a problem.

After 2:30—when schools began to let out—about 80 percent became negative. Students demanded to know how we could "invade [their] privacy" and "single out" specific students.

We did neither.

The whole point is that the Web is not private. If we can see it, anybody can see it.

And we didn't single out specific students. We used no names. In some cases, the references were relatively narrow, but still generic: Schools have a dozen or more cheerleaders.

Unfortunately, one example wasn't what it appeared to be.

The mistake, cited over and over again in e-mails and Web postings, didn't change anything: The girl holding a sign and flipping the bird was not actually a Hoban cheerleader but a picture of someone else the Hoban cheerleader placed among her personal pictures.

Is there any real difference? Isn't she sending the same message?

You can be sure a prospective employer wouldn't differentiate—which, as it turns out, is yet another risk you take in revealing yourself to the wired world.

Witness this note from a man in Texas: "Our firm always checks on MySpace and Facebook before we interview candidates so we can search for any information that may be useful in selecting—or de-selecting—them for our sales positions. . . .

"We have uncovered a tremendous amount of embarrassing, incriminating and illegal activities. If these children and adults only knew how much harm they were doing to their employment possibilities."

The writer was Scott Wollenberg, vice president of IMG Financial Group in Houston. He grew up in Sandusky and has relatives in Wadsworth and Norwalk, so he tries to stay abreast of the news in northern Ohio, including on our website.

The fact that a financial guy in Houston was one of the first people to respond to a newspaper article in Akron speaks volumes.

These kids seem to have no concept that something you put on MySpace at age 16 could come back to bite you at age 22, even if you're in Houston or Seattle or Timbuktu.

Not only is the Web everywhere; it's forever. Pulling down your site doesn't guarantee that somebody hasn't already made copies.

Yet another MySpace minefield was illuminated by a reader who repairs personal computers.

"MySpace is THE most troublesome place on the Internet for contracting virus and spyware infections," says Eddie Vidmar of Akron.

"The home pages have embedded music that you cannot stop from launching, and the XML [Extensible Markup Language] used underneath MySpace has been well-documented as a place for hackers to hide malicious code.

"I have a customer who constantly gets e-mail replication and Trojan-horse virus infections because her kid uses MySpace. So even beyond the trashy content the punk kids put on their page, it is actually harmful to the computer."

No kidding. After I surfed MySpace for less than an hour the other evening, my Webroot SpySweeper software caught 11 different spy cookies that had been secretly downloaded onto my computer. Cookies such as "AdRevolver," "Tribal Fusion" and "Advertising.com" not only compromise your privacy but also slow down your machine.

Another swell development: Scammers have figured out a way to post "new friend requests" on a person's home page that lead to porn sites. MySpace devotees have encountered a wave of that activity during the last couple of months.

Mind you, MySpace isn't inherently evil. Many—maybe most—area students maintain sites that are neutral at worst and uplifting at best.

A student from Firestone High who wanted to be identified only as Ayeshia said: "Not all teens on there have blatant, rude things. [The ones who do] can make it bad for the whole bunch."

At least one educator agrees.

Stephanie Scourfield, a teacher at Jackson High, assigned her Advanced Placement Language and Composition students to create MySpace sites. She forwarded addresses for a dozen student sites, including ones devoted to combating eating disorders and driving drunk.

"Not all teens are into self-destructive, disruptive behavior," she said. "Some have surprisingly mature social consciences."

Still, as one reader pointed out, any teen who spends time prowling MySpace in search of friends' sites is immersing himself or herself in an endless stream of profanity and alcohol glorification, creating a subtle form of peer-group pressure.

And then there are parents who sound like they need to go back to school.

"Most of the stuff these teens say is for show," wrote one mother. "I have no problem that my son has a pot leaf background and my daughter says she is so sexy. It is harmless fun.

"You took it way out of context and you had no right putting up their personal quotes for thousands to read."

As opposed to the millions who can read it online?

Jan. 30, 2007

Some Cops Are Superhuman

My jaw, like many of yours, took a plunge last week when I read a story on the front page of my favorite newspaper.

It essentially said that five of the state's six Supreme Court justices believe every police officer in Ohio has superhuman talents. Their eyes and training are so good that they don't even need radar or laser guns to figure out how fast you're going.

The court actually ruled, in the case of a Fairlawn man ticketed in Copley, that the cop's observations alone were sufficient for a conviction.

My reaction: If a typical cop can consistently come within 1 or 2 mph of judging the speed of an oncoming car, as a Barberton prosecutor claimed in court, I have greatly underestimated the human race.

I figured cooks had good use for measuring cups, and scientists actually needed those test tubes with the lines, and meteorologists tended to rely on thermometers, and pilots put their faith in altimeters, and baseball scouts made good use of their radar guns.

Well, apparently I underestimate the human race—or at least a well-trained portion of it.

This week, I rang up the Akron Police Department's traffic guys and basically said, "Prove it."

They did.

On Thursday, one of Akron's Finest took me out to shoot radar and laser beams at passing vehicles. The experience was an eye-opener.

Veteran officer Richard Stammitti has been training new officers in both radar and laser use since 1997. As part of their final test, they have to estimate the speed of 10 vehicles from a stationary position and 10 more while moving. To pass, the average difference between their estimate and the actual speed must be 3 mph or less.

Stammitti says a lot of the trainees quake at the thought of taking the Visual Speed Determination Test, but with practice, it's not that difficult.

We hit the road Thursday morning. After pulling into a special police lot on East Market Street, where officers start each shift by checking the accuracy of their equipment, we cruised around to a number of different locations, shooting at vehicles coming and going, while moving and stationary, with both radar and a laser.

At one point, we pulled over under a tree in front of the Joy Park allotment on Kelly Avenue. As I held the radar readout where he couldn't see it, Stammitti eyed the oncoming vehicles and estimated their speed, assisted only by the pitch of the tone emitted by the radar unit.

In 10 attempts, he came within 2 mph seven times. He came within 3 mph nine times. His worst estimate was 4 mph too high.

Average difference between his estimate and the actual speed: 1.8 mph.

That's impressive.

"The public thinks we're guessing," he says. "It's not a guess; it's an estimate. The reason it's an estimate instead of a guess is that, No. 1, we're trained, and, No. 2, we do it every day."

But get this: Stammitti is among those who think the court decision was misguided.

"I think the judges were trying to go in the right direction," he says, "but I think they went a little bit too far in saying, 'Everybody can just do this.' Well, everybody can't.

"There are times when I see a guy who I say is doing 48 and he's doing 45. It's a 25 mph zone. Does it really matter whether I got that exact number? The point is that he was speeding.

"I think that's what [the judges] were trying to say. 'Yeah, this person's speeding.' . . .

"[But] to say we can all do something—whether it's reporting, police work, fireman, I don't care what it is—you're going to have people who can, and you're going to have people who can't. And to include everybody makes it a little wider than it should be."

A similar thought was expressed by the court's only dissenting justice, Terrence O'Donnell.

He said the conclusion of his peers was too broad because it "eclipses the role of [a jury or judge] to reject such testimony," which, "if found not to be credible, could, in some instances, be insufficient to support a conviction."

Fortunately, that viewpoint seems prevalent outside of the court-room. Following a public outcry over the decision, both Republi-can and Democratic legislators have vowed to introduce bills this fall to require that technology be involved before a person can be convicted of speeding.

Not that technology solves all problems. Even when an officer relies on a properly functioning radar unit, judgment is involved.

On busy roads, the readout hops from vehicle to vehicle, finding its way to the largest object, perhaps locking on a slow-moving truck while a motorcycle speeds by. The newest radar guns will lock onto the fastest speed, but even then police must be able to judge by sight which vehicle is moving faster than the others.

"It's not an exact science," says Stammitti.

With a laser gun, it's much easier to pinpoint one vehicle. But the laser's range plummets in bad weather, and lasers don't work as well with trucks and vans. They also require a less-cluttered field of vision.

"They're each a good tool," Stammitti says. "You can't ditch one and say, 'I'm just going to use this.' Each have their own purpose, sort of like a car and a truck."

The overriding issue here, though, is a community's—or an agen-cy's—philosophy. In some places, speed enforcement is done in the name of safety. In many places, it clearly is done in the name of revenue.

Akron has a reputation for being reasonable.

Although nothing is carved in stone, Stammitti advises his train-ees to cut drivers some slack, giving them 5 mph in school zones, 10 mph in rural areas and 15 mph on the expressway. If you're whipping in and out of traffic, though, those parameters shrink considerably.

His bottom line: "If you're going up Route 8, doing 67–68 mph, going with all the traffic, not weaving in and out, you're fine."

Well, at least as far as the APD is concerned. But the APD isn't the only agency patrolling the state highways, if you catch my drift.

June 11, 2010

Romping at the Playboy Mansion

LOS ANGELES: Airbrushed? Like hell.

Anyone who doubts the authenticity of the architectural marvels in Hugh Hefner's life has never visited the Playboy Mansion and met a centerfold.

Rough assignment, I'll admit. But journalism is a calling. I was called.

They didn't have to call twice.

If you are among those who believe the whole Playboy empire is hopelessly politically incorrect, you are welcome to stop right here. But try to view this as a tour of historical import. The Playboy Mansion is, after all, the sexual equivalent of Dearborn and automobiles. Or Cooperstown and baseball. Or Broadway and the American theater.

Except this place is closed to the public.

The Playboy Mansion West, home to Hefner and his bunnies since 1971, sits hard by Beverly Hills in an even more upscale enclave known as Holmby Hills.

You hang a left off Sunset Boulevard and go past a couple of fenced-in palaces to a driveway with a big iron gate. Once the guard lets you through, you turn right, head up a steep hill, past some "Children at Play" signs, and park near the black Mercedes limousine with the license plates "HMH 1."

OK, I can already hear you asking: "Bob, how the heck did you get inside the Playboy Mansion?"

Well, I was just passing through town, gave Hef a buzz, and he said, "Hey, old buddy, I'll send a driver right over." Yeah, that was it.

Actually, I was in L.A. with a bunch of television writers. Playboy invited the group to a news conference to talk about Hefner's cable TV operation, the Playboy Channel. Several dozen writers—of both genders—took advantage of a rare opportunity to visit the Mecca of male hedonism.

That's the boring part. Here's the good part: While everyone else was dining inside a patio tent, your intrepid reporter went exploring. That's how he met Miss March.

She hasn't come out yet. I mean that in the publishing sense. She should hit the newsstands in mid-February. But more on her in a minute.

The first thing you encounter when you head into catacombs leading into what is known as the Beach House is a bank of safe-deposit-box-style lockers. You store your stuff and take a key attached to a big cord you can wear around your neck. Then, presumably, you are free to romp naked without worrying about losing your valuables.

Off that first hallway you find a series of really cool bathrooms with open showers and oak lockers. The bathrooms look like little caves, with stone walls and flagstone floors.

At the end of the hall, you see an opening in the floor that reveals a tightly wrapped spiral staircase. Take it and you wind up in an incredibly plush workout area, complete with treadmills, Stairmasters, weight machines, a ballet floor, walls of mirrors and the kind of ridiculously expensive audio and video equipment featured for the past four decades in the magazine.

That would be the magazine men buy for the articles on audio and video equipment. Yeah, that's it.

Off the main workout area is a room with tanning beds. Through another door is a big, tiled steam room. But perhaps the most amazing thing you see in the whole workout area is a sheet of paper containing a list of the mansion's telephone extensions.

To get the tennis courts, for example, you dial 246. The main swimming pool has three phone numbers. Not only do all six bedrooms in the Main House have phones, two of the *closets* do.

You also can call the "Film Vault," "Animal Department Back Cages," "Gardening Department" and "Scrapbook Research."

In all, your fingers can walk through 94 phone numbers and never leave the property.

I know there are 94 because I counted them. I was just finishing up when Miss March walked in.

Kimberly Donley of Scottsdale, Ariz., saunters into the gym, plops down on one of the brown leather couches and starts thumbing through the newly released February issue of the magazine, apparently checking out her competition.

She is not only predictably pretty but pleasant and very coopera-
tive. In a journalistic sense.

Miss March is wearing a blue work shirt, white corduroy jeans,
light brown leather boots and long, long, long blond hair. She also
is appropriately pneumatic.

She admits to being 27—a bit long in the tooth for a new Playmate—but looks much younger. "I'm the Den Mother of the
Month," she jokes.

These days, bunnies of any age are scarce at the mansion. The
1989 news reports seem to have been accurate, those reports that
had Hef's new wife, former Playmate Kimberly Conrad, cleaning
out the hutch.

"The girls don't hang out like it's one big party anymore," says
Miss March.

Asked whether Mrs. Hefner is responsible, she says she doesn't
know, but that, if so, "I don't blame her."

Miss March volunteers that Hefner's second wife is "a really great
person" and "a really dedicated mother" to their two children, ages
1 and 2½.

Mom is 30. Pop is 66.

Miss March is staying at the mansion because she has a video
shoot the following day. Miss April is living here, too, gearing up
for some work of her own.

The former has been around for a while because the photographer was trying to fatten her up. Seriously. He wanted her to gain 10
pounds. That assignment was not terribly difficult, given the mansion's 24-hour-a-day chef (in addition to full-time butlers, electri-
cians, drivers, gardeners, et al).

The fattening-up process now complete, Miss March will arise at
the decidedly unerotic hour of 5 a.m. to start shooting the 20-minute
video that is part of the standard centerfold contract.

Shooting the magazine photos took three weeks, including a full
week just for the one centerfold shot. She posed at a number of locations around town, including the Los Angeles Fencing Academy,
"because I fence."

Very lifelike.

Miss March got into the bunny business after a friend gave her name to a Playboy photographer. The reaction of family and friends? "My mother's thrilled," she says without a trace of sarcasm.

She says she has run into actors James Caan and Scott Baio at the mansion. And Atlanta Braves star Dave Justice had stopped by earlier the same day.

Then Miss March is off to get her beauty sleep. And your trusty reporter is back on the prowl.

As he leaves the Beach House, he encounters a plainclothes security guard with a walkie-talkie, and wonders whether Hef subscribes to the Frank Sinatra School of Media Relations. But the guard actually encourages the visitor to wander.

"Sure," he says. "Just don't go in the front door of the Main House over there, because Mr. Hefner and the family are relaxing. But you can check out the Game House over there. Or the Aviary over there. . . . "

The Main House is styled after a 14th-century Gothic-Tudor castle. Its Great Hall is said to contain originals by Matisse and Dali.

I pass the house and head into a huge English garden with stone walkways and statues. In one corner, largely hidden by landscaping, three huge satellite uplinks stand ready to beam Playboy entertainment into the cosmos.

In the distance, downtown Los Angeles twinkles through the misty night.

Over at the deserted Game House, 15 pinball and video games ring a pool table. A piano and scads of electronic toys beckon as well. Off the main room, in a small bedroom, is a circular bed. Unoccupied.

The Aviary is incredible, resembling a scaled-down version of the Cleveland Zoo's new RainForest exhibit. In addition to ferns, ferns, ferns, there are monkeys, exotic fish and huge, talking birds, including a macaw.

Yes, I talked to them. Nobody else was around.

Hef's six-acre spread also contains a two-bedroom Guest House, a Grotto with a long and winding swimming pool, a more traditional outdoor pool and what Playboy contends is the largest grove of redwood trees in Southern California.

Built in 1927 by the founder of the Broadway Department Stores, the estate is, by almost any standard, an incredible playground.

Ever see the famous sidewalk stars on Hollywood Boulevard? What a letdown. Ever visit the Pro Football Hall of Fame? Major disappointment. Niagara Falls? Tacky. But the Playboy Mansion exceeds all expectations. It's even cooler than you can imagine.

Still, something is not quite right on this rainy Wednesday night in January.

With its silent game room, its almost-deserted exercise room and its animals-only aviary, the Playboy Mansion seems a little bit too much like a museum, like some aging monument to pleasures past.

At one point, feeling guilty about missing the formal presentation, I return to the tent. But the talking heads at the podium could just as easily be from ABC, CBS or CNN. Or, for that matter, Procter & Gamble. They discuss marketing strategies, demographics, revenues vs. costs. . . .

So I sneak out again. Soon I discover a large sauna with big wooden benches. Although I have never been inside it before, I recognize it from magazine pictures. Pictures with hot, steamy, glistening Playmates.

But on this January evening, the heat is turned off. The sauna is vacant. The only thing inside is . . . a little . . . toy . . . stroller.

Talk about a cold shower!

In retrospect, maybe it was just an off day at the mansion. Maybe things pick up when the weather improves. Or the weekend rolls around.

Maybe we just need a little more research. Yeah, that's it. More research.

Hey, Boss. . . .

Jan. 24, 1993

Getting Pickled

Some athletes can play with pain. Others take a powder at the first sign of discomfort.

Now, I'm not saying Beacon Journal food writer Lisa Abraham is a wimp. But she did scratch herself from the starting lineup last week merely because of a sinus infection.

Abraham was scheduled to be a judge at a pickle-tasting competition at Lock 3 Park in downtown Akron. That's where the judging of various foods has been taking place each week during the Downtown Akron Partnership's farmers market.

In Abraham's defense, the woman cares more about food than most of us care about our firstborns, and she wasn't about to skew the contest results by partaking with a diseased palate.

Fortunately, she was not sufficiently impaired to stay home from work, so all she had to do was walk across the newsroom to find a fill-in.

And who is the first person you think of when you're looking for someone to nibble on your pickles?

Exactly.

As a last-minute replacement—well, she could have done infinitely better. I have been known to intone "hold the pickles" when ordering a burger, and my own food-preparation expertise ranges from PB&Js to boiled hot dogs.

But I am nothing if not a team player. So instead of fabricating an excuse, I decided to focus on pleasant pickle experiences in my past and suit up for battle.

If nothing else, I figured, I would be able to declare at some point that a particular pickle was "to die for"—a phrase that, for reasons that continue to mystify me, can be used only in connection with food. Nobody ever wants to die for a tee shot or a guitar riff or a watercolor.

But we digress. We were talking about my pickles.

With a hoarse voice that surely was channeled from her hooky-playing days back in grade school, Ms. Abraham offered some parting words of wisdom: "Don't be too easy. Don't be afraid to be the East German judge."

She told me that pickles should be somewhere between hard and "smooshy," and that sweet pickles should be sweet but not cloyingly so, and that dill pickles should be dill but not puckeringly so.

Or something like that. It all kind of blends together in the aftermath of consuming 18 different pickles, some of them multiple times.

In a couple of cases, I felt like Andy Griffith and Barney Fife being forced to sample Aunt Bee's "kerosene cucumbers." But most of the offerings were reasonably tasty.

My fellow judges were Dave Lieberth, Akron's deputy mayor, and Alan Medvick, a magistrate in Summit County Common Pleas Judge Mary Margaret Rowlands' court.

The pickles were presented in four groups: dill, sweet, hot and "other." Each pickle was to be graded on "visual appeal," "texture" and "taste."

"Visual appeal?" I asked. "I guess I never really looked at pickles that way."

"Wow, that's a very beautiful pickle!" quipped Medvick.

"Nice seed placement!" chimed in Lieberth.

As for "texture," the deputy mayor offered this explanation: "When your pickle is flaccid, you've got trouble."

Wouldn't know about that. But I'll take his word for it.

In all four categories, two of the three judges tabbed the same pickle as the best, so those were instantly declared the winners. My vote was part of three of those victories, which means one of two things: I'm a better pickle picker than I thought, or the other judges are equally clueless.

I'm betting on the latter. In fact, I'd be willing to bet you a gigantic gherkin.

They're to die for.

Aug. 27, 2012

Warning: Do Not Eat This Column!

The federal agency charged with protecting us from evil manufacturers has come to the rescue again.

The Consumer Product Safety Commission announced last week
that it has persuaded seven vending-machine firms to stick warning
labels on their machines.

Not just new machines, but the 1.7 million machines already
sitting around the nation's lunchrooms and gas stations.

A typical label will say: "Warning! Never rock or tilt. Machine
can fall over and cause serious injury or death."

Apparently, this is far from obvious. If it were, implies the commission, 37 people would not have died doing that very thing since
1978. And 113 more would not have been injured.

Statistics were not immediately available on how many of the
victims were seeking free pop and how many were exacting retribu-
tion on a machine that had gobbled their quarters without producing a pop. But it is safe to say these frustrated consumers allowed
their emotions to interfere with their logic.

Now, I know a lot of people who wouldn't qualify as Mensa
members, and every last one of them is aware that bringing an enormous object down on top of oneself can lead to complications. So
I'm not sure a warning label would have prevented this series of
unfortunate events.

What's next? A requirement that flagpole manufacturers include
warning labels about not sticking your tongue on the pole in subzero
weather?

Actually, we're almost to that point right now. Take a look at the
instruction manuals sitting around your house and you will see vivid
evidence of the impact lawsuits have had on the writers.

I personally possess an owners' manual for a General Electric
dishwasher that says: "Do not sit on the dish rack of the dishwasher."
Call me overeducated, but that strikes me as relatively self-evident.

As a reality check, I summoned my 5-year-old daughter, Kimmie,
and asked whether I should sit on the dish rack of my dishwasher.

"No," she replied, laughing.

Why not?

"Because it will break!"

Granted, Kimmie is a smart kid. But she's only 5. And one would think a person with the financial wherewithal to purchase a dishwasher would at least have the savvy of a 5-year-old.

Kimmie and I grabbed a tape recorder and went on a tour of owners' manuals. Consumer Product Safety Commission, listen up:

Should you put bottle caps, tin cans and aluminum foil in your garbage disposer?

"No."

Why not?

"Because it will break the thing."

Why shouldn't you put fingers or hands in the garbage disposer?

"Because you could cut yourself."

What would happen if you put your refrigerator on a floor that wasn't strong enough to support it?

"It would go through the floor."

Should you spill liquid in your video camera?

"No."

Why not?

"Because it will break."

Should you take your stereo out in the rain?

"NO!"

Why?

" 'Cause it will get ruined and not work anymore."

Should you stick tape on your CDs?

"No. Because they wouldn't work when you put them in."

If you have a snow blower, should you put your hands and feet under the rotating parts?

"What are rotating parts?"

They go around and around.

"No. 'Cause you can get run over."

You should put your feet under a lawn mower?

"No. Because you can get cut. A very bad cut."

Why shouldn't you drive your lawn mower onto the road without looking?

"Because you can get run over by a car."

Should you back up your lawn mower without looking for children?

"Unh-unh. 'Cause you'll bump into them."

Are these pretty simple?

"Oh, yeah."

Nov. 10, 1999

THE SPORTING LIFE

St. V-M vs. Hoban: Common Ground at Last

That it happened at all is amazing. That it happened during a game between two of the bitterest rivals in local high school sports is almost miraculous.

The bad blood between Archbishop Hoban and St. Vincent-St. Mary isn't quite on the order of Sunni vs. Shiite, but it is sufficiently intense that several years ago Hoban stopped scheduling St. V-M in several sports largely because of ugly incidents involving fans, players and coaches.

These days, the Lady Knight and Lady Irish basketball teams meet only in postseason tournaments, where the pairings are out of their hands. And that's what brought them together last week in a district semifinal game at Lake High School.

The favored team, Hoban, had a nine-point lead midway through the fourth quarter, thanks largely to its 5-foot-10 senior star, Tenishia Benson.

But St. V-M still had a chance Wednesday, thanks to its own 5-foot-10 senior star, Kara Murphy.

With 3½ minutes left, Murphy went up for a shot, came down awkwardly and bumped her head on the floor. A Hoban player tripped over her, then righted herself and ran down the court. Murphy stood up and tried to run, too, but couldn't move. She grabbed the back of her head, went down on one knee, then lay on the floor.

Her spill didn't look particularly severe, and Murphy is known as a tough, physical player, so most spectators figured she'd shake it off within a couple of minutes. But a couple of minutes turned to five, then 10, then 15. Clearly, something was seriously wrong.

Tenishia Benson had never met the injured player. In fact, she didn't know any of the St. V-M players. But she saw another human being in big trouble, and she thought about what she always thinks about in difficult moments: the power of prayer.

Benson gathered up her teammates and led them over to the St. V-M bench. The Hoban girls and the St. V-M girls formed a circle, joined hands and recited the Lord's Prayer. Then they did it again.

Benson was pleased, but thought even more prayer power was required. So she stepped away from the circle and—arms extended, palms up—urged the crowd to stand and join them.

The spectators rose in waves. Pretty soon, all 1,000 people were standing. The words rattled through the rafters: "Our Father, who art in Heaven. . . . "

At that moment, two warring schools became one.

Up in the stands, Hoban's boys basketball coach, T.K. Griffith, was standing next to his sixth-grade daughter. He turned to her, motioned toward Benson and said, "Look at her and want to be like her in every way. That's a leader."

Those present will remember the group prayer far longer than the basketball game (which Hoban won). And most of them will recall the skinny, bubbly girl who made it happen.

"I think I was directed to do that," Benson says now. "That was my job that night. Not to score points, but to make sure we remember that God is everywhere, and God is in everything. I think that was my job."

Benson says she hopes people will remember not the fact that she initiated the group prayer, but that it happened, and that it was "a unified spirit that allowed us to reach God and make sure she was OK."

She was eventually OK, but that wasn't immediately clear. Murphy lay on the court for 33 minutes before an ambulance arrived and she was carried out on a stretcher.

She spent four nights at Akron Children's Hospital with a Grade 3 concussion and a concussion of the spinal cord. But she is expected to make a full recovery.

One of her visitors the day after the game: Tenishia Benson.

So they really let you in Kara Murphy's room wearing a Hoban letter jacket?

"Oh, man," she answers, laughing, "we had to go through a strip search."

Benson has big, brown eyes, an expressive face and, despite

wearing braces, a ready smile. She's a solid student and a piano player who has accepted an athletic scholarship to the University of Cincinnati.

Murphy, who has accepted an athletic scholarship to the University of Akron, should be back at full speed in four to six weeks. Her mom, Pam, said Monday that Kara is still suffering from dizziness, weakness and tingling on her right side, but that doctors say the problem is swelling and bruising rather than structural damage.

Pam Murphy said her daughter was buoyed not only by Benson but other unexpected visitors—including a freshman from Revere— and by a "prayer chain" with messages of encouragement from the St. V-M student body.

As Murphy heals, Benson continues to field praise, some of it from unlikely sources. One of the spectators that night later took pen in hand and wrote, "I am a Walsh mom, but I hereby declare myself your fan." The woman lauded Benson for her "caring spirit."

When Benson opened the letter, in history class, she cried.

Her emotions were far different over the weekend. On Saturday, Hoban won the district championship by beating another big rival, Walsh Jesuit. Benson and her mates will play in the regional semi-final Wednesday in Ontario.

But more importantly, both Hoban and St. V-M are still buzzing over the amazing grace of a charismatic young woman who may have single-handedly restored a rivalry to its proper perspective.

March 6, 2007

Home Plate Covers All the Bases

Most stories have two sides: the official version and the truth.

Here, at long last, is the real story about what happened to home plate after it was dug out of the ground at Cleveland Stadium following the last Indians game in 1993.

Home plate did not go directly to Jacobs Field. It did not pass go. It went to a house in Akron's North Hill.

Then it went to a house in Springfield Township.

Then it went to a house in Green.

Then it went to a house in Uniontown.

Then it went to another house in Green.

Three days later—after hordes of Summit Countians had gotten their picture taken with home plate and/or put it in their yard and slid into it—the Indians finally got it back.

The story can now be told because the owners of the limo company who were entrusted with home plate no longer own the limo company.

"The Indians knew where it was," insists former limo owner Paul Zehner.

In general, yes. But team officials certainly didn't realize Zehner's stewardship would be quite so active.

"I never knew that!" exclaims Cleveland Indians Vice President Bob DiBiasio when asked about home plate's Summit County sojourn.

At the time, Zehner was a co-owner of Pegasus Motorcoach. The company offered the Indians two limos for the showy closing ceremony, held immediately after the final game on Oct. 3, 1993.

The postgame hoopla included speeches, a ceremonial last pitch, the introduction of current and former players and a customized rendition of *Thanks for the Memories* by former Clevelander Bob Hope. The climax of the one-hour affair came when members of the grounds crew, dressed in tuxedos and tennis shoes, climbed out of a limo, dug up home plate and placed it in the limo's trunk.

According to the party line, home plate would be taken directly to Gateway, where it would be used for one game before being shipped off to the Baseball Hall of Fame in Cooperstown, N.Y.

Well, one out of three ain't bad.

Home plate was indeed used for the first regular-season game at Jacobs Field on April 4, 1994. But the rest of the story doesn't hold Gatorade.

Tribe officials decided they didn't want to surrender such an important artifact to the hall of fame. The old plate has been on display ever since inside the Team Shop on the main concourse at Jacobs Field.

That's no secret to Tribe fans. But the route it took there might come as a shock.

First stop: a parking space near the Crazy Horse strip bar on St. Clair Avenue in Cleveland. That's where the two limo drivers had arranged to rendezvous after one limo dropped off Hope and his wife at the former Stouffer Tower City Plaza Hotel.

The drivers and their helpers got out, popped the trunk and stared in amazement. Then they showed some passers-by, who were suitably awed.

From the Crazy Horse, home plate went to North Hill, where Zehner showed it to his cousin, Don Zehner, and half the neighborhood.

Next was Springfield Township, where buddy Chris Madrin lived. Two additional stops were made in Green, to show cousin Mark Zehner and a buddy, Jeff McCort.

"I called everybody I knew," says Paul Zehner, laughing.

Among those who swooped down along the way was Mike Stull, deputy director of social services for Summit County. Stull, a pal of Zehner's North Hill cousin, attended the final game and had just settled in at home when the phone rang.

"Don called up and said, 'Mike, you want to see home plate?' " recalls Stull. *Of course* he did.

"There's all these neighborhood kids in the house, holding the plate, putting it down, sliding into it," says Stull.

"It was amazing to see it sitting there like some kind of holy relic or something. It sure as hell wasn't. That home plate caused me a lot of anguish over the past 49 years—you know, the players who didn't make it home and the ones who did."

But despite the Indians' long history of losing, people see magic in the old hunk of rubber.

"We all got our pictures taken with it," says Stull. "It was like sitting on Santa's lap or something."

Most of the time, the plate was stashed at Paul Zehner's house in Uniontown. And that first night, as he was watching the late sports report on TV, "I hear about how home plate was dug up and 'taken to a safe place.' And I said, 'Yeah. It's under my bed.'"

Zehner says he seriously considered carving his initials on the bottom, but chickened out. "I did break off a little clay and put it in a baggie that's in my sports room."

After three days, the precious platter was driven back to Cleveland and handed over to a team official, who merely said thanks.

The final game at Cleveland Stadium clearly is one of the highlights of Zehner's life. When his limo picked up Hope in the seventh inning, he was nearly speechless.

"I grew up watching Bob Hope on TV," says Zehner, 44. "When I saw him walk up, it was like watching God."

Zehner eventually introduced himself, with much trepidation. "I was worried. What you see on TV and what you find is sometimes two different things. But he was just the nicest man you could possibly meet."

Speaking of Hope, Zehner would like to lay to rest another myth in connection with that final game: Hope's hopeless senility.

None of the 72,390 fans who watched the old entertainer struggle with new lyrics to *Thanks for the Memories* realized that Hope hadn't seen the customized lyric sheet until moments before the song. "It wasn't his fault. He didn't get the new words until he was on the field."

Zehner's days of hanging out with celebrities are over. His family recently sold the limo company to concentrate on an auto repair business that's been in the family for 50 years.

He and his pals will no doubt be pleased to learn that the Indians harbor no ill will.

"I remember those guys," says Tribe Vice President DiBiasio. "We had a lot of fun and they treated us great."

The bottom line, DiBiasio says, is "no harm, no foul."

Dec. 11, 1996

'Akron Blast' Misfires

We've had nearly a week to come to terms with the new name for Akron's minor-league baseball team. And you know what? It's still hopeless.

Naming a team "The Blast" in honor of someone who died in an explosion is the stuff of Jay Leno monologues.

Already, people are coming from miles away to witness this grotesque freak show. Yesterday afternoon, Columbus television reporter Lorin Schultz and a videographer arrived at Canal Park to do a story. It wasn't a story about Akron getting a minor-league team. It wasn't a story about Akron's new $31 million ballpark. It was a story about blatant insensitivity.

Schultz, an Akron native, had no trouble selling her bosses on the tale even though Akron is well outside the Columbus viewing area.

"When I took it to the news meetings, everyone said, 'They named it *what?*'" said Schultz. "Our executive producer said, 'This is sick!'"

So last night, viewers all over Columbus were treated to the stranger-than-fiction saga about a baseball team that decided to "honor" fallen astronaut Judy Resnik with a team named The Blast and a mascot named Kaboom.

Schultz, who works for Columbus' Channel 4, the NBC affiliate, is a Firestone High and University of Akron graduate. Her parents, Bill and Marie Schultz, still live in Fairlawn. And as Schultz stood on the beautiful field under a bright October sun, she talked about being "thrilled" with the new ballpark.

"Too bad it's tainted now," she said.

That reaction is almost universal—in spite of what team owner Mike Agganis is saying.

With the possible exception of Sir James Goldsmith's raid on Goodyear, I can't recall another instance during my 12 years at the Beacon Journal when public opinion has been this one-sided.

Granted, last week's Beacon Journal telephone poll was not scientific because the participants were not selected randomly. Social scientists say the kind of people who will pick up the phone and voluntarily respond to a survey don't necessarily think the same way as people who won't. But in this case, the numbers are overwhelming. The Blast was given a thumbs-down by 2,400 out of 2,700 voters—a disapproval rating of 89 percent.

Eighty-nine percent!

And the phone keeps ringing. The mail keeps coming. The talk shows keep talking.

Many folks are expressing shock that the name could have gone so far awry. In a letter to the editor in Monday's newspaper, Akron resident Peggy Weaver inquired: "How in the world did the marketing group ever come up with something so insensitive?"

I'll tell you how.

Agganis hired a firm based in Minnesota. Those people never set foot in Akron. They never talked to anyone in Akron. They don't know the first thing about Akron.

All they had to do was ask. But they didn't. They never took any surveys or ran any focus groups.

The marketing people apparently got out an encyclopedia, looked up Ohio, and saw references to the space program.

Neil Armstrong . . . John Glenn . . . the Wright Brothers.

Unfortunately, Armstrong grew up in Wapakoneta—167 miles from Akron.

Glenn is from New Concord—80 miles from Akron.

The Wright Brothers were from Dayton—191 miles from Akron.

This is not Ohio's baseball team. Ohio doesn't need a baseball team. Ohio has a major- league team in Cleveland and another in Cincinnati. It has a AAA team in Columbus.

This is Akron's team. And Akron's connection to the space program is tenuous at best.

Agganis forced the connection, and everything turned sour.

There's still plenty of time to patch things up. As columnist Terry Pluto noted yesterday, fixing this would be easy. All Agganis would have to do is call a news conference, stand up tall in front of God and country and proclaim: "I goofed. I just didn't think it all the way through. Let's try again."

That's all it would take to turn this public-relations catastrophe into a legendary come-from-behind victory.

Oct. 16, 1996

October is the Cruelest Month

MIAMI: Somebody once compared the baseball season to a person's life.

The spring is short, exciting and filled with youthful promise. The losses are few, and insignificant.

Before you know it, spring gives way to the long summer, the workaday grind, a numbing routine that seems to stretch out indefinitely.

Then, toward the end, there's the crisp, desperately short autumn—a time of keen awareness that things are drawing to a close, that you have one final opportunity to make your mark, to get things right.

Even in the 80-degree heat of Miami last night, you could see the frost on the baseball pumpkin.

The playoffs are a baseball team's last stand. That's when a particular group of players either soars into sports immortality or goes quietly into the night, soon to vanish from the collective consciousness.

Put another tombstone in Northeast Ohio's sports cemetery. A big one. One for a postseason that lived a long and full life, but couldn't quite fulfill its apparent destiny.

Marlins 3, Indians 2.

Daylight-saving time is over—in more ways than one. The long, dark season is upon us again.

Will it be forever thus for the Cleveland Indians?

Miami's lovely weather teased us, hinted that maybe we could edge back that clock a little, at least slow it down enough to squeak out another incredible comeback in a marvelous, overachieving season.

With 80 degrees on the thermometer after a sun-filled day, the evening seemed as full of promise as any this season. You had the feeling the Indians had a great chance to get it right for once.

Just once.

But as of 12:05 this morning, it may as well be snowing in South

Florida. The good vibes were merely our brain cells rattling around from all the deafening salsa music.

No, the season wasn't a complete waste.

Stephanie Zahler of Canton, who watched both games here, is not ready to toss herself into the Atlantic. She scoffed at the idea that the season was just another exercise in futility.

"No! No!" she said. "They're awesome. I'll be ready again next season."

We do have some gold-leaf memories.

We'll talk about Jaret Wright, the incredible kid pitcher who started the year at Canal Park in Akron, wearing a purple uniform with "Aeros" across the chest.

We'll feel warm when thinking about this refreshing collection of friendly guys, guys who were far easier to root for than the surly players of the recent past.

We'll smile when we think about the Big Socks.

But such talk won't transcend generations. At least not as a World Series would have.

This one hurts.

In October, every game is etched in stone. And this headstone has the score backwards.

Last night's action in front of 67,204 at Pro Player Stadium also has taken its place in hundreds of thousands of memory banks. But that place is the part of the brain that handles short-term memory.

Can you believe this?

How can this keep happening?

How can we go through the same thing year after year after year?

Apparently, the Gods of Baseball are very, very, very angry with us.

First, they make us wait three decades to get a decent team. Then they curse us with a players strike. Then, for two years in a row, they curse us with a playoff system that forces the team with the better record to play its first two games on the road.

Maybe it really is time to get rid of the Chief Wahoo logo. Or maybe merely getting rid of Herb Score will lift the jinx next year.

But who can think about next year yet again? Who can think of anything other than that gnawing pain in the gut?

Well, Don Baker of Canton can.

"We beat the Yankees, we beat Baltimore, we got to the seventh game," said Baker, 39. "It's a high. It's been a good time, a fun ride."

Nor was Bill Martin overly discouraged. The former Barberton schoolteacher, now living near Columbus, viewed last night's contest as a way to get in touch with his late father.

Martin was flashing back to the 1948 Series, which he saw in Cleveland with his dad.

"I can still remember where we sat," he said. "I even remember where we parked."

Mind you, this was 49 years ago. A World Series win can have that kind of impact on a person.

Maybe this veteran Indians fan has a better perspective. Maybe we should be happy just to be here.

"For a team to get in the World Series is much more difficult (than in 1948) because there are more teams," he said.

Former Cleveland Heights resident Peter Marx, 45, whose parents live in Macedonia, came from his home in Tampa because "absolutely nothing was gonna stop me from going to this game." And even this bitter Tribe loss couldn't sour Marx on the '97 Tribe.

"They got a real mix and chemistry that will go on for years," he said.

Many others were relatively sanguine as well.

"It's wonderful just to be here," said Melodie Waltz, a former Painesville resident who now lives in Cape Coral.

Easy for her to say. She doesn't have to go back to winter and stay inside for the next six months and stare at that big, empty, dusty trophy case.

Oct. 27, 1997

Field Tilted Toward Private Schools

Only 8.5 percent of Ohio's high school students attend parochial schools. But of the 10 Ohio schools that have won the most sports championships, 70 percent are parochial.

Parochial schools have won 31 consecutive Division I titles in wrestling, 21 straight in boys swimming, 10 straight in volleyball, seven straight in ice hockey and five straight in girls basketball.

In the big-money sport, football, church-affiliated schools have won 22 titles in the 36-year history of the state playoffs—a whopping 61 percent.

Why the huge discrepancy? Simple: The playing field is not level.

Private schools assemble virtual all-star teams from five- and six-county areas, while public schools must make do mostly with whoever happens to reside within the boundaries of their school districts.

Do private schools go around recruiting the best athletes? They're not supposed to, and they insist they don't. But they are allowed to recruit students in general, and if one of those students happens to be the best football player in the region, well, an admissions office generally won't object.

Part of the reason so many stars end up at parochial schools is that kids and their parents want to be involved in strong athletic programs. Therefore, a lot of this is self-perpetuating.

And for some families, a religious education is paramount. Their only decision is which private school to patronize.

But the reasons this happens are less important than the fact that it happens.

The bottom line is that interscholastic tournament competition in Ohio is horrendously disproportionate and intrinsically unfair.

Walsh Jesuit, a Catholic school in Cuyahoga Falls that has been in existence 43 years, has won 33 state championships and six national championships.

Seven of the seniors on Walsh's 2006 national-championship girls soccer team earned athletic scholarships to Division I colleges. Here's where each of the seven resided while at Walsh:

- Rose Augustin (University of Notre Dame) lived in Silver Lake.
- Kathleen Callahan (Miami) lived in Brecksville.
- Amber Kasmer (Wright State) lived in Euclid.
- Darcy Riley (Wisconsin) lived in Bath.
- Liz Secue (Purdue) lived in Bath.
- Kelly Thomas (Loyola in Maryland) lived in Shaker Heights.
- Daniella Vespoli (Miami) lived in Bath.

These folks have every right to go wherever they want, of course. But imagine how good the Revere soccer team would have been had those three future Division I players from Bath played for their local school. Revere didn't even get out of the district tournament—little wonder, with their top players siphoned off.

That same year, Walsh sent a 6-foot-4, 285-pound lineman to national football power Boston College. Nick Schepis commuted to Walsh from North Royalton.

The Beacon Journal's 2007 Tennis Player of the Year was Walsh's Nate Hobrath—who lived in Strongsville.

A surprising number of public school stars wind up hopping to private schools as upperclassmen. One of the best female sprinters in America, Aareon Payne, spent her first two high school years at Ellet in Akron. Then, after winning the state 200-meter championship as a sophomore, she transferred to Beaumont, a Catholic school in Cleveland Heights—45 minutes from Akron.

The year she arrived, Beaumont's girls just happened to win their 15th state track championship.

Payne, now a senior, has accepted a full athletic scholarship to Southern Cal.

When the girls basketball coach at Medina County's Highland High was pushed out midway through last season, the team's star player, Jackie Cook—who was leading the Suburban League in scoring with 23 points per game—suddenly quit Highland and enrolled at Regina, a Catholic school in South Euclid.

That would be the same Regina that ended the regular season ranked No. 1 in Northeast Ohio by the Plain Dealer and reached the final four in Columbus.

Never mind that Regina—a tiny Division III school—is 34 miles from Highland High.

Cook wasn't eligible to play for Regina this season, but by mid-January, she was already sitting on the Regina bench, wearing a Regina sweatshirt with her old Highland number (22) on the back.

Which brings up a key point: Unequal competition doesn't just happen among the biggest schools. Private school dominance is just as noticeable in the smaller divisions.

In girls basketball—the top sport for females—parochial schools have won six of the last 10 titles in Division II and eight of the last 10 in Division III.

In soccer, the boys and girls combined have five divisions. During the last two seasons, private schools have won eight of those 10 titles.

Wrestling has three divisions. Parochial schools have won not only 31 straight in the biggest division, but also nine straight in the smallest division.

The solution? Simple. Create two state tournaments, one for public schools and one for private schools.

Let the two continue to compete during the regular season—many public schools relish the challenge of taking on a local all-star team, and public schools have achieved some noteworthy upsets—but when it comes to the postseason, put the apples with the apples and the oranges with the oranges.

The idea is not new. In Maryland, New York and Texas, public and parochial schools play separate tournaments. But the Ohio High School Athletic Association shows no signs of moving in that direction.

Two years ago, a committee was formed to investigate what could be done to balance the scale. According to OHSAA Commissioner Dan Ross, the committee came to the conclusion that the growth of open enrollment among public schools had begun to equalize the competition.

In addition, he said, the consensus among those on the panel—superintendents, principals and athletic directors from both public and private schools—was that winning an all-inclusive championship is more meaningful.

"There was a very strong feeling that all of the schools together make a stronger tournament," Ross says. "If you're going to win a state championship, you want to win it with everybody being involved."

Ross, a graduate of St. Charles High, a parochial school in Columbus, points out that 74 percent of the state's 662 public school districts now offer some type of open enrollment.

On the other hand, a quarter of those schools offer open enrollment only to residents of adjacent districts. And, according to figures from the Ohio Department of Education, 73 percent of all public school systems had a net gain of 25 students or fewer this year counting all grades. Not exactly a flood of outsiders.

The assertion that open enrollment has evened things up is laughable to many of us, including the athletic director of a local public school that itself offers unlimited open enrollment.

"The playing field is not level," says Stow Athletic Director Cyle Feldman, who thinks the state needs two playoff systems.

"Here's a great example: Our community was so excited about going down, a year ago, to the state girls basketball tournament [in Columbus]. And we played Cincinnati Mount Notre Dame. We looked at their roster, and their kids were from everywhere."

Stow's girls were blown out by 20 points.

"I said to my coaches, 'Congratulations—you're the public school champions.' I meant it.

"That bothers me."

Stow has won five state titles, more than most schools but far fewer than the majority of Summit County's parochial schools.

The athletic director at the area's winningest school agrees that schools like his have an edge.

Walsh's athletic director, Grant Conzaman, does not favor a split playoff system, but he readily acknowledges that private schools are on the better end of a tilted field.

"To say it's level would be overstating it," he says.

"I know there's the underlying thought that private schools can get kids from all over, which we do. That's not a question. My only objection [to the common perception] is that there's nothing nefarious that we're doing. We're just trying to get kids to come to our school."

Although public schools complain that they often lose their best athletes after the eighth grade, Conzaman notes that public teams are usually made up of kids who have played together for many years and don't need to adjust to new teammates.

But he concedes that the staying-together factor pales in comparison to the six-county factor.

"My private school colleagues will probably bristle if they see this in print," he says, "but what the heck—it's true."

As Lake High School Athletic Director Bruce Brown points out, recruiting isn't necessarily a dirty word, as long as it's done by the book. The book says athletes can't be offered anything more than any other student.

"The reality of it is, parochial schools were developed as recruiting tools for the diocese," Brown says. " . . . That's how they make their livelihood.

"If I'm a private school, I've got to recruit people to come or I'm out of business. So I kind of chuckle anymore when people say, 'They're out recruiting.' Well, of course they are! That's what they do!"

Brown is not ready to endorse a split system, though.

"I would not suggest at all that it's totally balanced," he says, "but I don't know in the big picture if it would be the healthiest thing to separate public and private schools from a tournament standpoint."

To be sure, public schools aren't immune to rolled eyeballs when a stud player's family decides to relocate.

Future Ohio State University signee Justin Zwick made a national name for himself while playing quarterback at Orrville High—then showed up at legendary football power Massillon Washington.

Stephanie Gibson, the starting basketball point guard for Kent State University as a freshman, played for Copley until eighth grade, then ended up at perennial power North Canton Hoover, which had just won a state championship.

Her former Hoover teammate, Brittany Orban, the Beacon Journal's 2008 Player of the Year, spent her entire childhood playing for Green.

Still, these are exceptions. The vast majority of parochial athletes don't live where they play.

When it comes to fairness, something clearly is amiss—and not just in Ohio. Athletic associations all over the country have been trying to address the same issue.

Half a dozen states use a "multiplier" system that forces smaller parochial schools into bigger divisions. In Illinois, for example, if you have 100 boys in your school, you must multiply that by 1.65, giving you an enrollment of 165 boys for the purposes of determining your playoff division.

In Arkansas, the figure is a hefty 1.75. The lowest is Missouri's, at 1.35.

But multipliers can create other inequities, and multipliers do nothing to change parochial-school dominance in Division I, which is our state's biggest problem.

Tim Flannery, assistant director of the National Federation of State High School Associations in Indianapolis, is a graduate of Cleveland powerhouse St. Ignatius. But he has lived the equation from both sides and knows things aren't equal.

"I was the athletic director at North Olmsted, and I will tell you that [a multiplier] doesn't help big schools that are public. You're still going to play Ignatius or [Cleveland's St.] Ed's. I don't care how many times they multiply."

Parochial schools have two other advantages:

- Alumni and boosters provide massive amounts of money for athletic facilities, uniforms and travel. At Walsh, this year's booster-club budget is $204,000. Most public schools don't raise one-quarter of that amount.
- Private schools can offer scholarships. At Walsh, 25 percent of the student body gets help with the $9,200 annual tuition.

Put those two factors together and you get results such as this: Had LeBron James gone to his local high school, Kenmore, rather than accepting a scholarship to St. Vincent-St. Mary, he never would have been able to travel to places like Los Angeles and Philadelphia to play the best high schools in the nation.

So the parochial dominance marches on. This school year—in all sports, in all divisions, both boys and girls—8.5 percent of the student population has won 47 percent of the state titles.

The imbalance is actually getting worse, not better. Says Flannery, from the national association: "Having been raised in a Catholic setting, the big change in the last 20 years is the fact that non-Catholic kids go to parochial schools. And there's nothing to stop that.

"That didn't happen back in the '60s. You went to Catholic grade school, you went to Catholic high school.

"And this is happening across the country, in every state."

As Flannery notes, any attempt to solve the problem is certain to ruffle feathers.

"Very few of our states have been able to come up with a solution everyone's happy with."

In this case, the majority seem a lot less happy than the minority.

May 19, 2008

Why Play Sports?

An English professor at the University of Akron took note of the hubbub surrounding a couple of columns I wrote about fairness in high school sports and declined to join the fray.

He was interested in a far more basic question: Should high school sports exist at all?

Thomas Dukes, Ph.D., offered an intriguing counterpoint to our collective obsession with sports.

"For some of us academic types, sports are, at best, only tangentially related to the academic enterprise. (Let me add that many who feel this way were terrible at sports in school, suffered greatly in gym classes designed for those who didn't need such classes, and no doubt require intense therapy over the experience.)

"Given the very limited resources devoted now to what I'll call 'classroom education,' I was wondering if you could tell me why sports should be part of education.

"I read an essay by Carl Sagan once that claimed young men battling on the athletic field were essentially engaged in a civilized form of re-enacting battles to expend their energy, and I'm aware of the mythic argument (football teams as warring armies, etc.).

"I'm still trying at my ripe old age (52) to *get* sports, especially team sports. I once e-mailed [legendary sportswriter and National Public Radio commentator] Frank Deford, who suggested I ask an academic. Of course, I am an academic."

Well, if it makes you feel any better, professor, I will admit that a part of me is embarrassed to be a hard-core sports fan. The emphasis our society places on sports is absolutely absurd, and I have contributed more than my fair share of publicity.

But that being said, I do think team sports offer a number of extremely valuable benefits to the participants.

At the risk of incurring the cosmic wrath of Carl Sagan, the idea that young men are war re-enactors is a bit of a reach—especially considering the number of young women now immersed in team sports.

I love the fact that girls are into it, too, because they can derive exactly the same educational benefits. To wit:

Learning how to work with others toward a common goal.

Learning that the amount of effort you put into something often translates into how well you do.

Learning to sometimes sacrifice your own goals and ego for the common good.

Learning to work side by side with people who aren't like you, people you normally wouldn't associate with.

Learning to perform in front of an audience.

Learning to stand behind your mates, even when things go bad.

Best of all, realizing that, when you lose, when you've played terribly, when you've tried your best and it wasn't good enough and your world is in the dumper, you can come right back another day and turn everything around.

Sports also keep kids in good physical condition, keep them off the streets and, in a world that is dominated by shades of gray, give them a nice psychological outlet: The playing field is a place where the outcome is absolutely clear. There's a scoreboard. You either win or you lose.

How many times in life do you get an indication of exactly where you stand?

Sports also can provide the sheer joy of mastering a skill, the same joy one would derive from learning to be an accomplished pianist or sculptor.

Unfortunately, most of the fans are far more focused on other things. And that's where sports go wrong.

Don't blame the game.

June 5, 2008

Wounded Tiger Doesn't Hurt Firestone's Zoo

Almost everything has changed, but nothing has changed.

Since Tiger Woods last grabbed a championship trophy at Firestone Country Club—a mere two summers ago, although it seems much longer—he has acquired a new caddie, a new swing coach, new management, new injuries, a new reputation and a new vulnerability.

He lost his wife, badly tarnished his golden-boy image and dropped like a boulder in the World Golf Ranking.

But the man still triggers a frenzy wherever he goes.

Immediately after the announcement Thursday that he would make his long-awaited return from the disabled list at the Bridgestone Invitational in Akron, requests for media credentials shot up.

Keep in mind that most news organizations plan trips well in advance to save money, and the dates for this tournament have been set for more than a year. Yet just since Tiger tweeted his intentions, 18 more news organizations and 30 more reporters have signed on.

That brings the total media attendance to 367 reporters from 125 organizations and nine countries.

Seriously.

To watch guys play golf.

On Tuesday morning, a lot of those folks showed up just to hear guys *talk about* playing golf.

Well, one guy.

At precisely 9:53 a.m., seven minutes early, Woods strolled into the interview room looking dapper, if a bit monochromatic, in a black Nike cap, a dark gray Nike shirt and dark gray slacks.

Anyone who expected the 35-year-old legend to seem sheepish after sitting out nearly 12 weeks with knee and Achilles' tendon injuries was in for a surprise. Except for a new configuration of facial hair, which makes him look a bit like a Cablinasian Amishman, he seemed like much the same fellow as the one who made his Firestone debut in the final year of the previous century.

Woods was relaxed and confident, often funny, occasionally pointed and always articulate. (How many professional athletes use words like "volatile?")

Questions flew in all sorts of different accents, no surprise given the presence of sports hounds from Australia, Japan, Germany, Britain, Ireland, Scotland, Canada and Korea.

Even if the leaderboard no longer changes much based on Tiger's presence or absence, the overall atmosphere certainly does.

Larry Dorman, veteran golf writer for the New York Times, looked around the media workroom early Tuesday morning and said, "I've been here on Tuesday before, and I've never seen as many people in this room as I'm looking at right now.

"There's always a different vibe when Tiger's around. Now it's different in a way; before, you were there to see if he was going to win, and now you're looking to see how he's progressing. It's caused by a different thing, but it's still a Tiger kind of buzz."

ESPN's Tom Rinaldi was among those whose plans changed because of Tiger. He was scheduled to cover another event this week but was redirected at the last minute.

Unlike past years, the course was closed to the public on Tuesday, mainly because the number of fans paying to watch practice rounds two days before the actual competition has not been large enough to justify the cost of staffing the grounds, particularly in terms of security.

But even that changed after Senor Woods decided to come.

"We definitely ramped up our security," said Akron police officer Mike Gilbride, stationed at one of the entrances. "We were not supposed to be here today. When they found out Tiger was coming, they wanted an additional four officers."

Twenty-nine minutes after entering the media lair, Woods exited Stage Left. Just outside the door, he was ambushed by the always amiable Bob Stevens, a former Cleveland TV sports anchor who now lives in Hilton Head, S.C., and works for the PGA Tour Network.

A few Q and A's later, Woods climbed into the back seat of a silver Cadillac CTS 4 with Michigan plates and sped off into the bright summer morning, allegedly sound of both body and mind.

We'll see.

Aug. 3, 2011

The King Builds His Castle in Bath

The surprise is not that he's building a huge house—What, you expected LeBron James to buy a bungalow on a land contract?—but that 19 local families will be living within 800 feet of his bedroom window.

Most of those people are wondering why. They can't figure out why a guy who could easily afford hundreds of acres and complete privacy would build his dream house in the middle of their relatively modest Bath Township neighborhood.

They started wondering that in 2003, when LeBron paid $2.1 million for a house there.

They really began scratching their heads two years later when he knocked it down to clear the way for something bigger and better.

Much bigger and much better.

According to the blueprints, LeBron's new home will encompass 35,440 square feet.

That's a tough number to wrap your mind around, because the township's next biggest house (formerly occupied by ex-Telxon boss Raymond Meyo) is a mere 13,914 square feet.

Let's put it this way: LeBron's home will be closer in size to the Montrose Best Buy, which is 45,000 square feet.

The basketball star's pad won't be finished until the summer of 2008—and no wonder. It will include a recording studio, a two-lane bowling alley, a casino, a 26- by 63-foot theater, a sports bar, an aquarium and a barbershop.

Yes, a barbershop. Says so right there on the prints. Lower level. Near the front. Next to the bowling alley.

A first-floor master suite, which includes a two-story walk-in closet, is about 40 feet wide and 56 feet long—bigger than half the houses in Bath.

A place like this does not have a "dining room." It has a dining *hall* (roughly 27 by 27). It not only has a "great room" (34 by 37), but a bigger, two-story "grand room." The "family foyer" off the six-car garage—near the elevator—is inconsequential compared to the "grand foyer" inside the front entrance, complete with a sweeping, divided staircase leading up to four second-story bedrooms.

Outside, the west wall will feature a limestone sculpture—a bas-relief of LeBron's head, wearing his trademark headband.

The exterior is contemporary, with varying roof lines and angles. Thanks to architect Robert J. Porter III, it doesn't look nearly as massive as you might expect.

Bath Zoning Inspector Bill Funk says the home didn't require a single zoning variance—although a previous owner got special permission to raise the maximum see-through fence height to 8 feet.

Construction began in August. The house is under roof, but plenty remains to be done, including the exterior walls.

LeBron's place will not initially include two staples of the rich and famous: There's no indoor basketball court and no swimming pool, at least for now. Space has been saved for a large outdoor pool with a kiddie pool and a pool house. Another future addition: a mammoth garage.

LeBron's lot is an oddly shaped, 5.6-acre tract wedged among lots that average 2.3 acres and houses that average 3,209 square feet. His property is 300 feet wide at the street and 677 feet deep. About two-thirds of the way back, the width expands to 471 feet.

One of the cornerstones of wise home-buying is that you don't want the most expensive house on the street. But when your income hits nine figures and you're hanging with the likes of Warren Buffett, all the traditional rules go right out the window. You build exactly what you want, and you build it where you want it.

Clearly, LeBron is more concerned with another real estate axiom: location, location, location. He's within easy striking distance of his office (also known as Quicken Loans Arena) and on the outer fringe of his hometown.

"It lets me be close to my family and friends in the Akron area and continue to contribute to the community," he said through his agent.

The house is in the southern part of the township, not far from state Route 18. We're not going to provide a TripTik, because traffic already has been a major headache for the neighbors.

"People who come to photograph it are disrespectful," says Tom Bader, one of LeBron's nine immediate next-door neighbors.

"They park their car in the middle of the street—with their doors open! And you're sitting behind them! All I wanna do is go home after a hard day's work."

Sometimes Bader even has to wait to turn into his own driveway because gawkers have driven up into it, hoping for a better view of LeBron's place.

"As far as LeBron the man goes, I think he's an outstanding individual," says Bader, a graduate of James' alma mater, St. Vincent-St. Mary High School.

"He's great for Cleveland. I'm proud to have him. I have no issues with LeBron James at all. The problem is the baggage that he unintentionally carries with him."

Of course, living next door to one of the most popular athletes on the face of the planet is something plenty of people would love—especially young ones.

"My children obviously think it's cool," says Bader, laughing. "They can hardly wait to go over and play basketball with him.

"I said, 'Honey, I don't think that's going to happen. Besides that, don't ever, ever invite LeBron over to our house to play ball because he's going to twist his ankle and I will have my house eternally egged.' "

Another neighbor, who didn't want to be identified, said most of the residents, being typical Cleveland sports pessimists, figure LeBron eventually will leave for greener pastures, and they fear nobody else will be able to afford the place.

"Our concern is, if he leaves Cleveland, what is going to become of this home, this monument?" she said. "What would it become if it weren't going to be somebody's home?"

Well, when you're in LeBron's financial ballpark, you could keep it as a summer house.

In fact, he's already juggling multiple residences. While he waits for his palace to be finished, the best player in Cleveland Cavaliers history is splitting his time mainly between a huge apartment in downtown Cleveland and a relatively modest four-bedroom house in Medina County's Highland school district. He paid $580,000 for that one in June 2005.

And to think that only five years ago this guy was living with his mother in a two-bedroom flat at Spring Hill Apartments, a subsidized-housing complex next to the Akron Expressway.

The Bath house LeBron bought in October 2003 for $2.1 million ($1.1 million in cash) and then demolished was not exactly a fixer-upper. It was a 12,611-square-foot, 11-bedroom mansion that once belonged to Telxon boss Robert Meyerson.

The property has an interesting history. In the late 1980s, it was the modest home of two schoolteachers, Dan and Sandy Boarman, who still teach in the Copley district. Dan doubled as the head football coach until resigning this year to take the head football job at—yes—St. Vincent-St. Mary.

During the 1990s, the house was bought by a dentist who later sold it to Meyerson, who started adding rooms faster than most families add magazines. By the time LeBron bought it, Meyerson had turned it into one of the most expensive homes in Summit County.

Then—*poof!*—dust.

And now this.

As superstar houses go, LeBron's design is not particularly eccentric. According to Sports Illustrated, San Antonio Spurs star Tony Parker and his flame, Desperate Housewives actress Eva Longoria, have a special room in their home set aside exclusively for . . . their . . . dogs.

March 27, 2007

Your Kid Won't Go Pro!

I'm not a sportswriter, but I play one on TV (occasionally).

I'm not a professional athlete, either, but I played varsity sports in high school and college, and my kids have played in high school and college.

So I've been around the sports block. And one of the things I have discovered makes me crazy: At least half of the sports parents in Greater Akron seem to think their kid will grow up to be a professional athlete.

Sorry. Not gonna happen.

If you're molding your family life around that goal, you need to call time out and look at some statistics.

Let's start here: Of all the boys in America who are playing high school football, a mere 5.7 percent will go on to play in college at *any* level, including Division III, where athletic scholarships are not permitted.

Of the precious few football players who *do* manage to land on a college roster, only 1.8 percent will be drafted by the National Football League.

Bottom line: If your kid is a high-school player gearing up for summer practice, the odds of him reaching the NFL are 0.08 percent.

You literally have a better chance of drowning—0.9 percent of the population—than of seeing your son on *Monday Night Football*.

And the football odds are considerably better than the basketball odds.

You think your kid is the next LeBron? Think again.

Out of the 546,000 high school boys on varsity basketball teams around the country, a mere 3 percent will ever wear a college uniform.

And if your kid beats those hefty odds, his chances of moving from college to the NBA are a mere 1.2 percent.

High school players who eventually turn pro? Try 0.03 percent.

His odds of being struck by lightning are 0.02 percent.

Girl basketball players fare about the same. Only 3.3 percent of the high-school ballers land on a college roster. That's *any* college roster. Forget Tennessee or UConn.

From high school to the WNBA? Same as lightning.

These statistics are courtesy of the NCAA, which, in its occasional lucid moments, likes to remind its starry-eyed "student-athletes" that getting a college diploma might not be such a bad idea.

Now, given these statistical realities, does it really make sense for the parent of a high-school player to pay astronomical fees to offseason travel teams that journey all over the country for tournaments, disrupting the entire family's daily existence?

OK, I hear you. A college education can easily cost $80,000. Who wouldn't want their kid to get one for free?

But do you want to stake your family's financial future on your child winning an athletic scholarship? Even if you do, is that fair to your kid?

One reason parents think the way they do is that some of the folks running AAU basketball programs, Junior Olympic volleyball programs and elite traveling soccer programs all but guarantee that Little Penrod or Penelope will win a "free ride" if he or she joins the program and gets "exposure."

Another problem is that, from middle school on up, too many school programs are geared to producing Division I college players.

Bruce Brown, athletic director at Lake High School and one of the most thoughtful sports administrators in the area, says high schools need to keep in mind the reality that hardly any of the kids on their teams will play in college.

Says Brown: "The charge I give our coaches and the message we're trying to get out there is, 'If we're just addressing those 3 percent, we all ought to be fired.'

"It's the 97 percent that we need to coach and work with and focus on."

Here's one more thing to ponder the next time you're daydreaming about mansions and Bentleys: LeBron isn't one-in-a-billion. Even if you only consider him to be among the top three players in the world, he's one in two billion.

Which leaves 1,999,999,999 who aren't.

June 17, 2008

Teasing Albert Isn't Funny

Is anybody else having trouble working up much sympathy for the guy Albert Belle hit with a baseball?

You know, the insensitive slug who made fun of Belle's alcohol problems, the problems that sent him to a rehabilitation program last summer?

That would be the 10-week program that was so wrenching, so intense, so personal that Belle emerged from it asking to be called by his given name, Albert, rather than his longtime nickname, Joey, to indicate the extent of his transformation.

In this day and age, every knucklehead in the stands ought to know that alcoholism is a disease, every bit as much a disease as cancer. Would the guy who loudly invited Belle to a keg party corner a chemotherapy patient and serve up a couple of one-liners about baldness?

I can hear the chorus already: "Hey, Belle makes $100,000 a year. He ought to be able to take a little heckling."

Yes, Belle—who is woefully underpaid by contemporary Major League standards—will make more money this year than a veteran school teacher will make in the next three. So what? Does that mean Belle is somehow non-human, that he's a legitimate target for absolutely any kind of verbal abuse?

The idea that professional athletes are superior to other human beings, that they have some kind of magical, bionic makeup, is responsible for a lot of the problems that infest pro sports—on both sides of the dugout. It is the reason, for instance, that people like Jose Canseco and Leroy Hoard think speed limits have nothing to do with them.

But the fans can be even more obnoxious. They think that just because they fork over $11 for a damn ticket they have bought their way out of even the most basic societal obligations.

I wasn't at the game in question. But I've sat next to plenty of guys like the clown who got hit. You can find them at any Indians, Browns or Cavs game—but most of them don't surface until the fourth quarter, after they've established a close relationship with the beer vendor.

Then, suddenly, they have all the answers.

The guys I sit near always seem to have spittle running out of the corner of their mouths as they shout out their inane comments, their eyes not so much on the player as on their fellow spectators, in gleeful anticipation of their reactions.

"Hey, Joey," the guy reportedly yelled on Saturday. "We're having a keg party after the game. Come on over!"

Belle, who was near the stands because he was chasing a foul ball, picked it up and fired it right into the man's chest from about 15 feet away.

You may have seen the poor, wronged fan. He was happily displaying his boo-boo for the TV cameras. He had become *somebody.*

And this took place at a home game! What happens on the road?

I'll tell you what. Things like this:

It is 1976, and the Browns and Steelers are playing at the Stadium. Because I am taking photographs for a newspaper, I am standing on the field, near the area now affectionately known as the Dawg Pound.

Steeler quarterback Terry Bradshaw drops back to pass. Joe "Turkey" Jones breaks through, picks up Bradshaw and slams him on his head.

As Bradshaw lies motionless after the play, a huge roar of approval cascades down from the stands. Team doctors run out and huddle over him. He still is not moving. Eventually, they call for a stretcher. For all anyone knows, Bradshaw is paralyzed for life.

As he is carted out on the stretcher, whiskey bottles, shot glasses and beer cans fly out of the bleachers toward him. Verbal abuse rains down from everywhere.

Apparently, spectators tend to view people like Bradshaw and Belle more as figures on a Nintendo game than real human beings. It's astounding.

OK, as a player, you can't throw a baseball into the stands, either. You could literally kill someone. And if your aim is off just a little, you could hit the wrong person—maybe some little kid.

So in the end, there probably is no real justification for Belle's act. He probably shouldn't have done it.

Helluva throw, though. Helluva throw.

May 14, 1991

LeBron Takes His Talents to South Beach

During most of May and June, a small yard sign was stuck in the grass across the street from LeBron James' mansion in Bath Township. The letters at the top read "MVP."

Upon closer examination, the sign was not a tribute posted by a neighbor, as you might assume, but an advertisement for a home-improvement company—Mahoning Valley Premier.

It has been that kind of year. Obvious signs that aren't. Great expectations and big crashes. Foreshadowings and red herrings. Smoke and mirrors and guessing games and gamesmanship and paranoia.

As of today, though, the picture, at long last, is crystal clear: LeBron James is gone.

Surprised?

If so, why?

This is who we are. This is what unites us. This is what keeps us grounded when residents of cities all over the country temporarily lose their bearings when the sports pendulum swings and their losers turn into winners, if only for one fleeting season.

As our first true superstar since Jim Brown dribbles off into the sunset, chalk up another year without a title—and, at this point, without much hope for the future.

We now have gone 16,479 days without a major sports championship.

As Fox TV's Chris Rose so aptly summed it up a few years ago, "Cleveland sports fans are 90 percent scar tissue."

As of today, I'd say we're up to about 95 percent.

This one is especially tough, though, because, this time, things really, truly felt different.

He was a local kid through and through, not another hired gun. Not a California-born CC Sabbathia, making no bones about cashing in on a gigantic New York payday, nor even Midwesterner Jim Thome, hinting he'd take a hometown discount before bolting to Philly.

This was LeBron Raymone James, born in Akron, raised in Akron, poor and obscure in Akron to rich and famous in Akron, a young man who never stopped expressing his undying affection for Akron.

What other MVP in any sport insisted on holding the trophy presentation at his old high school and, the next time around, at the hometown college where he played many of his high school games?

On the second day of May, on a drizzly Sunday afternoon, LeBron took the stage at Rhodes Arena (a half-hour late, as usual) and offered no hint that he was unhappy with his geography. To the contrary.

"The city of Akron means so much to me," he declared, national TV cameras humming.

"Akron, Ohio, is my home. Akron, Ohio, is my life. I love this city. . . . I love Akron, Ohio, to death."

Anyone who had viewed *More Than a Game,* the fine documentary on St. V's national championship team, thought LeBron harbored an inordinate amount of love for both his homeys and his hometown.

The movie is far less about LeBron than it is about a team and a city. It's a film about dancing with the people who brought you to the dance, of accomplishing far more collectively than you can individually. *More Than a Game* is a 100-minute testament to the rewards of loyalty.

Anybody who happened across LeBron at the Copley High School softball field last week also got the feeling this guy wasn't pining for the warm sand of South Beach. He and some pals, including Romeo Travis and Sian Cotton, gathered for a casual pickup game and later posed for photos with a bunch of youth baseball players who spotted them.

And so, it was with a fair amount of confidence that we got down on one knee and asked the prettiest player in the world for his hand—and he turned his back and walked away.

On national television.

The hurt and anger are magnified by the fact that this whole free-agent marathon became a national referendum on the desirability of Northeast Ohio.

Granted, LeBron ended up here only because of a random bounce of a lottery-night pingpong ball. But he never seemed like a mercenary, and he never suggested that images of greener pastures were dominating his daydreams. His fantasies consistently consisted of winning championships.

So we tried our best to ignore the fact that he proudly wore a New York Yankees cap and made no secret of his love for the Dallas Cowboys.

Had we listened more closely, perhaps we would have realized that our hometown hero harbors more love than a 1960s flower child. During this year's playoffs, he proclaimed his undying affection for no fewer than five other cities—not including Miami.

It was Chicago's young center, Joakim Noah, who jump-started the civic smack. After spending a between-games Sunday in deserted downtown Cleveland, Noah declared there is nothing to do here. He even added that Cleveland "sucks."

Despite being booed lustily, he didn't back down. In fact, he ramped things up. During a subsequent postgame news conference, Noah, wearing baggy black jeans, a crappy-looking sweatshirt and tennis shoes, said he didn't regret a word.

"I never heard anybody say, 'I'm going to Cleveland on vacation.' What's so good about Cleveland?"

Reporters couldn't wait to get LeBron's response, to perhaps goad him into taking a shot at Noah's city of employment. But when asked about Chicago, LeBron lit up.

"It's a great city," he said. "It is. It's an awesome city. Honestly. It's one of the best cities we have in America. Great restaurants. Great shopping. . . .

"I'm not trying to say this because of what [Noah] said about Cleveland. I'm dead serious. I think we all love Chicago.

"I go on vacation in Chicago sometimes. I do. You all are making it a joke, but I'm serious. I love Chicago. I love Cleveland. I love Akron, too."

After the Bulls were dispatched and the identity of the next opponent had been determined, your favorite columnist jokingly asked LeBron, "So . . . does the city of Boston 'suck,' or would you go there on vacation?"

LeBron laughed and sang Boston's praises.

"I don't know if I'd go there on vacation, but it doesn't suck. I have a good time when I'm in Boston. It has great restaurants. It's a great sports town. It's a great city."

And the love just kept on spreading.

He spoke reverently of the Big Apple, home of historic Madison Square Garden and financial capital of the cosmos.

And when CNN's Larry King asked him about the Los Angeles Clippers, LeBron offered this about LA: "It's a great city. It's a great city."

Is there any place this guy doesn't love?

Fueled by such comments, the speculation about LeBron's future became an American obsession. As CNN's King noted at the start of the NBA Finals, LBJ was "the most talked-about figure in sports in the United States."

The frenzy was so intense that a sitting president addressed the topic—more than once.

After initially telling sports announcer Marv Albert that he'd love to see LeBron in a Chicago Bulls uniform, Barrack Obama, in a sit-down interview with King, changed his tune: "I'll be honest with you—and my folks in Chicago may be mad at me for saying this—but I think it'd be a wonderful story if LeBron says, 'You know what? I'm going to stay here in Cleveland.' . . .

"That's a town that has had some tough times. For him to say, 'I'm going to make a commitment to this city,' you know, I think would be a wonderful thing."

The nationwide speculation turned comedic at times—and not just on the late-night talk shows.

The NBA has an "anti-tampering" rule that prohibits team officials from openly lusting after another team's player. Less than two weeks after Cleveland's quick exit from the playoffs, executives from three different cities already had been fined for their remarks.

The biggest blunder emerged from the active mouth of the Dallas Mavericks' maverick owner, Mark Cuban, who wistfully contemplated a "sign-and-trade" deal that would bring the Chosen One to Texas. Cuban was fined $100,000.

A co-owner of the Atlanta Hawks, asked whether he would give LeBron a maximum contract, replied, "In a heartbeat." Who wouldn't? Doesn't matter. He was fined $25,000.

The most absurd penalty was levied on former Cav Steve Kerr, who at the time was general manager for the Phoenix Suns. Clearly joking, Kerr said maybe LeBron would settle for his team's "midlevel salary exception," referring to a contract available to midlevel players. Steve now has $10,000 less to spend on fine dining.

In stark contrast, a bunch of other folks were *bringing in* money by joking about LeBron's future.

Late-night comic Jimmy Fallon, the day after Cleveland lost Game 5 to Boston, declared: "The Cavs suffered their worst home playoff loss in their history. But, to be fair, LeBron had to leave at halftime to shop for apartments in New York City."

David Letterman had an ongoing bit called "Reasons LeBron James should come to New York," and slipped him into a couple of Top 10 lists.

In "the Top 10 surprises at the Senate oil-spill committee meeting," this was No. 6:

"Half the questions were about LeBron coming to the Knicks."

On a Jimmy Kimmel show, actor David Spade quipped, "LeBron should stay in Cleveland because if he moves, he'll have to wait all day for the cable guy."

Other commentators didn't sound quite so hilarious to Northeast Ohio ears. The day after the first playoff loss to Boston, Rick Reilly told his ESPN audience that LeBron should bolt because the proper alignment of stars calls for Kobe Bryant in LA and LeBron James in NYC.

"LeBron in Cleveland is like Madonna in Wichita, Kansas."

Well, Toto, I guess we're still in Kansas.

If LeBron made up his mind a while ago, he did a marvelous job of hiding it. He has gotten extremely good at hiding his true feelings.

From the start of his career, he has subscribed to the Michael Jordan School of Marketing: Try not to alienate anyone; hold your emotions; answer all questions patiently and politely; and talk to the media even on days when you don't feel like it.

Unlike stars who won't talk before a game—Shaquille O'Neal among them—LeBron typically holds court about 45 minutes before taking the court. During the 10 minutes he sets aside, the media frenzy inside the Cavs luxurious dressing quarters bordered on slapstick.

The home team's locker room is glorious. It has a deep-blue carpet with a big Cavs logo cut into the center. The lockers are made of natural maple with stainless-steel accents. Each player has a bevy of audio/video equipment right in his locker, including an Xbox, a Bose sound system and an Internet port.

One of the clubhouse walls features three huge flat-screen TVs. On another wall is a door to the training room, a full-length mirror and a glass-doored refrigerator that contains eight different types of pop as well as bottled water, juice and energy drinks.

The remaining two walls are devoted to lockers. But night after night, the focus was squarely on the far-left corner—LeBron's locker.

Make that two lockers. The extra one gave the poor guy next to him, Anthony Parker, a tiny additional sliver of space to try to get dressed while radio, TV, newspaper and Internet reporters and videographers swooped down on the fellow who has the word "Chosen" tattooed across his back.

The swarming of LeBron mirrors what would happen if you told a group of 40 schoolchildren there's free candy in the corner. They rush forward, bumping into each other, jockeying desperately for position, reaching over top of each other to thrust tape recorders close to the mouth of The King.

After games, LeBron usually met the media in a big interview room down the hall, where the head coaches and stars of each game are trotted out on a high stage in front of five rows of padded folding chairs and a riser for television cameras.

After being crushed at home in Game 5 against the Celtics—an unmitigated disaster that saw literally half of the fans gone with five minutes left on the scoreboard clock—Cavs officials speculated that LeBron probably would be an interview-room no-show. But after slowly showering and dressing—then carefully checking his outfit in the full-length mirror—he marched down the hall to face the music.

The general tone of the questions was, "What the hell was *that*?" He calmly answered them all, his general thrust being, "Boston is good."

If you didn't see LeBron's defection coming, you're in good company. Even people who know him well were misled.

At the second MVP ceremony, his first high school coach, Keith Dambrot, was standing on the floor of Rhodes Arena, waiting with thousands of others for the big man to arrive.

Granted, Dambrot is not a member of LeBron's inner circle. In fact, LeBron initially was so steamed when Dambrot left St. Vincent-St. Mary for the University of Akron that he didn't know whether he ever wanted to speak to him again. But they patched things up long ago and still talk.

"I have no inside information," Dambrot said that day, "but if I had to bet my house one way or the other, I'd bet that he stays in Cleveland."

You'd figure Dambrot would know what makes LeBron tick. The coach has known the player since LeBron was only 13, a scrawny, 5-foot-11 kid showing up with a horde of other young boys and girls on Sunday evenings at the Jewish Community Center in West Akron, where Dambrot ran a weekly, no-nonsense basketball clinic—admission $1 per head.

Dambrot knew before anyone else that this product of inner-city Akron poverty was destined for greatness.

"He was like a sponge," said the UA coach. "Everything you said he absorbed. He just kept getting better and better and better, and he continues to get better and better.

"He's a basketball genius. As good as he is physically, he's better mentally."

But Dambrot's guess about LeBron's future came at a time when Cleveland was leading the Boston series 1-0—in other words, before LeBron started to look extremely human.

By MVP standards—and most certainly by the standards expected of the Savior of a City—the Chosen One bombed in the 2010 play-offs.

Against Boston, in stark contrast to his amazing series against Detroit three years earlier, No. 23 did not throw the team on his back and march it to the top of the mountain. Too often, he looked mortal. A couple of times, he actually appeared to quit.

And, for the first time, he absorbed some full-body public relations blows, including this one, from Yahoo sports columnist Adrian Wojnarowski: "Everything has come too easy to him, and he still doesn't believe that winning championships takes a consuming, obsessive desire that borders on the maniacal.

"He is . . . medicating his insecurities with unending and unfolding free-agent dramas. James is chasing Warren Buffett and Jay-Z the way he should be chasing Russell and Jordan and Bryant."

The following day, syndicated columnist Jason Whitlock unleashed this broadside: "Yes, we're all witnesses. We're witnessing the corrosive effects of money and fame on a young mind. LeBron James showed us another crack [in Game 5] with his passive-aggressive on-court tantrum meant to throw his supporting cast under a bus."

Even former NBA star James Worthy got in on the act. During the Lakers-Celtics championship series, Worthy—owner of three NBA championship rings—said LeBron would look like a "quitter" if he left Cleveland without any jewelry.

"My personal opinion," Worthy said, "is a lot of times when you lose and you leave, it sounds like a quitter. I would never want to leave without accomplishing the goal."

Are they right? Is LeBron considerably less than the Real Deal, or were those observers overreacting to a couple of rotten games?

We may not know for a while. But we do know that the rest of the basketball world desperately wanted this guy, and that he's a huge talent, and, unlike so many other of the world's most prominent athletes, he has kept his nose clean.

"You never know how guys will handle success and money," noted the old coach, Dambrot. "That's the thing you have to be most proud of—that he continues to work hard to try to become the greatest of all time, which is a possibility."

It certainly is. But if it happens, those of us living in Northeast Ohio will no longer be firsthand witnesses.

July 9, 2010

There Used to Be a Ballpark

Cleveland Stadium is not about Jim Brown and Rocky Colavito. Not really.

It's about Tom Muscenti.

Tom happens to be from Mentor, but he's a lot like you. He's a lot like me.

He could be any one of the literally tens of millions of Northeast Ohioans whose lives have been touched by the gigantic concrete-and-steel structure that has hugged the shores of Lake Erie for 65 years.

When I think back on the grand old ballpark—which is being dismantled and dumped into the lake to make way for a new facility—I will think first of Muscenti.

He was one of 72,390 people at the final Indians game on Oct. 3, 1993.

As usual, the Indians lost. They were shut out in the stadium's first game in 1932 . . . they were shut out in the stadium's last game in 1993 . . . and in between they lost a lot more often than they won.

But on that final day, nobody cared about the score.

When the game ended and the postgame ceremony began, not a soul got up to leave.

Ninety-year-old Bob Hope, unsteady and hard of hearing, shuffled onto his hometown field to sing *Thanks for the Memories*.

Members of the grounds crew, wearing black tuxedos, dug up home plate with a pick ax, put it in the trunk of a white limo and drove it south on East Ninth Street to Gateway, where it would stay for one game before moving on to the Baseball Hall of Fame in Cooperstown, N.Y.

Finally, after an hour of festivities, the affair was over, and the fans began to trickle out slowly, almost grudgingly. It was 5:30 in the afternoon. The sun had dipped most of the way behind the 115-foot-high roof on the third-base side of the diamond and now lit only the right-field stands.

This was the transitional sun of early October, a sun that is bright yet not fully here, a sun in the midst of changing from a throbbing, constant companion to a distant acquaintance.

Muscenti was still sitting out there in that sun. And tears were streaming down his face.

Here was a guy in the initial stages of middle age, a guy who noticed each morning in the bathroom mirror that his hairline was farther back than it was the day before.

Here was a successful financial planner—the career he had chosen after realizing he would be unable to make his living on a baseball field.

He was not exactly sobbing, but a steady trickle was visible, including a long streak down his left cheek.

Muscenti made no effort to hide the flow. He just sat there, looking straight ahead, blinking against the sun and the drops coming from his eyes.

Muscenti was thinking about his life. About how things used to be.

A long time ago—20 years—he had sat in this precise location with his mother. She had taken him by the hand and led him through the massive concrete concourse to the 1963 All-Star Game, the childhood equivalent of nirvana.

Although Muscenti now owned season tickets in a far better location, he wanted to sit out here for the last game because that's where he had sat with his mom.

Muscenti's mom was no longer around. She had passed on. He could no longer thank her for taking him to the game. He could no longer thank her for his magical childhood.

One time, many Octobers ago, this man was certain he would grow up to be a pro ballplayer. Every little boy thinks he's going to grow up to be a pro ballplayer. Or at least every little boy who grew up in the '50s, '60s and '70s.

Whadya mean it's a lousy field? Any Northeast Ohio kid knew Cleveland Stadium was the perfect field. The only field. It was arrow-straight foul lines of white chalk . . . a glorious expanse of bright-green grass . . . a dark-brown infield that was geometric poetry.

We loved Cleveland Stadium. We didn't have any other big league field to compare it to. The only thing we could match it against was the weed-infested diamond with the rusty wire backstop at our local school or park.

When we entered that oval behemoth and heard the hot dog vendors and smelled the cigar smoke and laid eyes on that 4.2-acre playing surface, we never wanted to leave.

These players were gods. Even when they were in seventh place.

We loved the way they moved, the way they held their bats, the way they pawed the dirt with their cleats.

When we got home, we'd grab a white T-shirt and a Magic Marker and draw the number of our favorite player on the back. Then we'd go outside and *become* that player.

The same thing happened during football season.

Every baby-boomer boy in Northeast Ohio at one time or another pictured himself as Jim Brown—unstoppable . . . uncatchable . . . unbelievable . . . running and running and running . . . flashing down the sidelines with No. 32 on his back as a cosmic roar rained down from 80,000 hysterical fans.

The heroes changed over the years, but the fantasies didn't. Little kids wanted to play like Otto Graham or Jim Brown or Brian Sipe or Bernie Kosar. The players were all connected, linked directly to a glorious heritage.

The early Cleveland Browns weren't merely good, they defined pro football. During their first 10 years of existence, the team named after Coach Paul Brown won seven championships.

It took a long time for things to turn sour. And it happened just about the time the town started going sour.

During the '70s, when Northeast Ohio had become a national laughingstock thanks to burning rivers and economic default, the championship tradition had faded badly. But these were still *our* Browns. We hung in there, taking a sort of perverse pride in riding out the storm.

A popular T-shirt at the time read, "Cleveland: You Gotta Be Tough." And nobody ever accused Cleveland football fans of lacking toughness.

This combination of football and baseball gave Cleveland Stadium a split personality.

Each fall, the gentle aesthetics of baseball gave way to the immediacy and brutality of pro football. And each football season was itself schizophrenic.

Early in the schedule, September sunlight would sparkle off the shiny orange helmets, which, along with the brown jerseys and white pants, would contrast gloriously with the rich emerald field.

But as the schedule wound down, the grass turned beige, the blue skies were obliterated by a permanent smear of gray and the arrogant winds of Lake Erie thundered around inside the big horseshoe, making everyone miserable.

That was pretty much the setting when the Browns won their last title in 1964. The 27-0 upset of the Baltimore Colts still stands as Northeast Ohio's last major sports championship.

The late-season weather always seemed oddly fitting. Football is a physical test, a competition of wills. You Gotta Be Tough. Think it's easy living in a Dawg Pound?

Somehow, when fans started ripping out whole rows of seats with their bare hands at the final Browns game on Dec. 17, 1995, their actions did not seem wholly inappropriate.

Owner Art Modell had wrecked the franchise, and now it was time to wreck the stadium.

Today, the stadium's work is done.

Yes, the place was built on a landfill. Yes, the sightlines were atrocious. And, yes, during its golden years, the playing field was a disaster and the plumbing was a joke.

But the yellow-brick monster was ours—rotting fangs and all.

A person simply couldn't live in Northeast Ohio for any length of time and not be touched by it.

This is not just another building that has outlived its usefulness. This place has been a symbol—both personal and communal—of our hopes and dreams.

But the trouble with dreams is this: Even if they come true, they don't last. Mel Harder can tell you about that.

Harder, like the tearful Muscenti, was at the final Indians game in '93.

The former pitcher was among the ex-players who ran onto the field during the closing ceremony in period costume—Rick Manning in the bright-red top of the '70s ... Max Alvis in the sleeveless jersey of the '60s . . . and onward back to Harder's baggy wool uniform with the big "C" on the front.

Many of the players had turned potbellied and gray. Some, like the 80-year-old Harder, had a difficult time even trotting onto the field.

In 1932, Harder had thrown the first pitch at the new stadium. Now, in a wonderful piece of symmetry, he was throwing the last pitch, a ceremonial final toss to a youngster who was waiting behind home plate.

Harder peered through his bifocals, wound up and heaved. But the ball landed short and bounced to the young catcher.

"I wanted to throw it 60 feet so bad," Harder said later. "But something happens to my arm about halfway through. It loses its power."

Age happened to your arm, Mel.

Age happens to all of us. It happens to the Mel Harders and it happens to the Tom Muscenties.

It even happens to the Cleveland Stadiums.

Dec. 1, 1996

Tune Out Penn State, Tune In Revere

Although you may not view Howard Stern as the unerring voice of truth and reason, on Monday morning he was dead-on: "Penn State students who miss their 'JoePa' need to have their heads examined."

Amen.

Penn State has set a new standard for athletic corruption, the most egregious example yet of the double standards involved in big-time college sports. Every last person on that campus who had even passing knowledge of the situation should be quartered.

But as these scandals continue to mount, it's easy to lose sight of something important: This stuff does not personify team sports.

By definition, everything that makes the national news is an aberration. If somebody goes to work, does a good job and drives home safely, that's not news. If he goes to work with an Uzi and mows down his colleagues, that's news.

Just as most people don't flip out and kill people, most coaches are the absolute antithesis of what we're hearing about Jerry Sandusky.

Nearly every high school and college coach I've ever encountered, both personally and professionally, is coaching because he or she loves the kids—and not in the Jerry Sandusky sense.

They love taking raw freshmen and molding them into confident senior leaders, all the while teaching lessons that will serve them well later in life—everything from time management to coping with adversity to working with others who aren't like you to learning that sometimes you have to sacrifice your individual goals for the common good.

Although I've never met a coach who didn't want to win every game, the degree to which they love their players is not dictated strictly by wins and losses.

Take a look at this year's football program at Revere High School.

Revere has enjoyed magical seasons in the recent past, but this wasn't one of them. Final record: 0-10.

A complete disaster? A waste of everyone's time? Not on your life.

Head coach Phil Heyn says his kids practiced just as hard during Week 10 as Week 1. But he is even more proud of what they did off the field.

Revere players were involved in youth-mentoring programs, litter cleanups, reading programs, yardwork for senior citizens, fundraisers for the Haven of Rest and Toys for Tots and a slew of other activities.

For every DMarques Jones, the St. Vincent-St. Mary player charged with raping and killing a 3-year-old, there are thousands of kids like Brandon Peterson, a Revere football co-captain with a 3.75 grade-point average.

Here, for the sake of balance, is a story about Peterson you'll never hear on any newscast.

A man from North Canton—a man Peterson had never met— took his two boys to Revere's game against Aurora. Revere got pounded, 52-21.

As the dejected Minutemen shuffled through the gate on their way back to the locker room, one of the man's sons stuck out his hand.

The rest of the story comes directly from a note the father (businessman Mike Eastman) mailed to the football player in care of the coach.

"Despite your obvious disappointment, you noticed my 6-year-old's outstretched hand. . . . Not only did you give him 'five,' but you looked him directly in his eyes and said, 'Thanks for coming.'

"It was such a small gesture that you probably don't even remember it. But I promise you my son does. As you walked away, he looked at me and said, 'That's my favorite player, Dad.'

"It is said that in times of adversity a man's true character is revealed. Continue to be the kind of person that can look into the eyes of a child and thank him for coming after a tough loss, and make his night like you did, and you will succeed in things much more important than football. . . .

"Thank you, Brandon, and hang in there—nothing worth having ever comes easy."

Which do you think Brandon Peterson will remember longer: the score of that game or the contents of that note?

A lot of student-athletes get excellent character-building lessons at home. A lot of them don't. And when they don't, their last best chance is often a coach.

Coaches don't coach for the money. When you add up all the hours a typical high school or small-college coach invests throughout the year, most of them make about 50 cents an hour.

So when you think of coaches, don't think of Jerry Sandusky. Think of guys like Phil Heyn, whose kids discover plenty to value even during an 0-10 season.

Nov. 17, 2011

READERS RITE GOOD

Bridge Over Akron, Akron, Akron

Bob: *Since moving to Lake Township from West Akron, I only recently had occasion to drive past the White Pond interchange at Interstate 77, where the new bridge boldly proclaims: AKRON AKRON AKRON AKRON AKRON AKRON AKRON AKRON AKRON AKRON.*

Who's idea was this? Did taxpayer dollars pay for it, or was it a free gift from the construction company? If it was a free gift, they should pay us, because it is tacky tacky tacky.

How about "Akron"? How about "Welcome to Akron"? How about "Akron—High-Tech City"?

Why the ugly color? Why the ugly font? Is this a cruel prank?

If the same construction company builds a bridge in Tennessee, does the bridge say, "CHATTANOOGA CHATTANOOGA CHATTANOOGA CHATTANOOGA CHATTANOOGA" because they can only fit five?

I think this idea is STUPID STUPID STUPID STUPID STUPID STUPID STUPID STUPID STUPID STUPID.

Many thanks for your tireless devotion to these issues.

Bill Jelen, Lake Township

BILL: You're welcome welcome welcome.

You are also one savvy motorist. It only took you one trip past the White Pond bridge for you to correctly identify AKRON TO THE TENTH POWER as an aesthetic disaster.

As another motorist wrote: "I thought it was just something temporary that they were going to paint over, like that church out in Fairlawn that had 'Go Tribe' on its roof while it was being built. Then I drove underneath it and saw that they were actually bolted onto the concrete. Lord, it's tacky."

Yet another observer says it reminds him of "a pair of college sweat pants."

The head honcho for the company that built the bridge, Jim Ruhlin of Ruhlin Construction, wants to make it clear the signs were not his company's idea.

"It was part of the original contract," he says. "We get a set of design plans . . . and that's what we bid."

Ruhlin's firm has built hundreds of bridges over the years, but this is a first. He has seen only one bridge that even approaches this concept: Near Columbus, over I-270, a wrought-iron railing contains multiple references to the town of Easton.

The Akron letters are plastic. To attach them, workers had to drill holes in the concrete, insert anchors and use stainless-steel screws. With 10 Akrons on each side, we're talking 100 letters.

Ruhlin said it is not possible to break out the exact cost of AKRON ETC., but estimated it was "less than $10,000."

Good lord.

The Ohio Department of Transportation also washes its hands of responsibility. Traffic management coordinator Jerry Jones says most of ODOT's rules cover physical obstructions created by signs, not aesthetics.

The buck stops at Akron City Hall. Spokesman Mark Williamson lays the blame on the desktop of service director Joe Kidder. He said Kidder wanted to emphasize the fact that White Pond is "the entry point for the City of Akron."

Yeah, but if you're northbound, you're *leaving* AKRON AKRON AKRON.

"Well, it's similar to a city limits sign."

Except they don't put up 10 city limits signs. Why not just have "Welcome to Akron" on one side and "Leaving Akron" on the other?

"Well, let's see. . . . People are driving so fast we don't want to worry about them actually reading something, so we give them the repeated image of Akron?"

Please note that Williamson was trying to stifle his laughter.

Fortunately, we have a sliver of hope hope hope. According to Ruhlin, some AKRONs could easily be removed "if there was an uproar."

Let's uproar. In the name of visual decency, I urge you to pick up the phone and call the service director right now.

Oct. 19, 2001

Scandalous Behavior

There's nothing funny about sexual harassment.

Well, hardly ever.

In this particular case, it's tough not to crack a smile.

Reader Dean Ab-Hugh, from the Wayne County burg of Apple Creek, notes that he might have some 'splaining to do if he ever runs for president, because he once was the target of a co-worker's complaint to Employee Relations.

"Many years ago," he writes, "I was at a company party in North Carolina, wearing my BALL-U shirt.

"A very militant and angry female accused me of sexism. I told her the shirt was from Ball State University, and my daughter (a recent graduate of BSU) had sent it to me.

"Angry female said there was no such place as Ball State University. She almost had me there; as a Bowling Green alumnus, I don't normally recognize the existence of Ball State.

"I suggested that she was free to go to Employee Relations and file a charge, but I wasn't going to take off my shirt. It had become a matter of principle.

"Angry female did go to Employee Relations to file a charge and (you'll never see this one coming), the lady she talked to was a graduate of Ball State University. Honestly, I hadn't known that.

"Well, actually, I was single, and I might have dated the Employee Relations lady a few times.

"But I never wore my BALL-U shirt thinking it was going to stir up a fuss.

"Charges of sexual harassment take many forms, and some of them are inconsequential."

PUZZLING MOVE

Speaking of potential sexual misunderstanding, I'm surprised at the new name given to an Akron citizens group.

The longtime club recently announced that it will henceforth be known as the West Akron Neighborhood Group.

They could have gone with, say, the Neighborhood Group of

West Akron, but no. In news releases they are proudly trotting out their new acronym: WANG.

TIMES CHANGE

Speaking of matters of the loin, a nice woman who works at my gym gave me a college textbook she used at Kent State in 1960 called *Modern News Reporting.*

Chapter 29 is devoted to covering sexually oriented stories. Early in the chapter, author Carl Warren bemoans the fact the typical young reporter is steeped in "the finer points of diplomacy, politics, economics and science," but is hopelessly naive when it comes to dealing with sex.

"It is perhaps small wonder that he flounders. Taboos and restrictions on the discussion of sex at home and in the classroom have limited his learning. He has never written an English composition or even a personal letter about sodomy or indecent exposure. He may be confronted with them during his first week at work."

Only secondhand, we would hope.

"If instructors and students include sex news as an essential topic for study and practice, such training will be a boon to city editors. . . . "

I couldn't agree more. If I could go back to school, I would definitely get in a lot more practice.

Nov. 8, 2011

Mangled Phrases Bring Joy

The other day, recently and a little while back, we were talking about redundancy.

We've done that more than once. And, thus far, the clear favorite is the sticker that graces gas pumps at Circle K stations all over Greater Akron: "Please prepay in advance."

Some other good ones are lurking out there, too, and Beacon Journal readers are having fun pointing them out.

Jim McIntyre of Cuyahoga Falls passed along this gem:

"Perhaps the ultimate redundancy is Arby's French dip sandwich that they advertise 'with au jus sauce.' Literally, that's 'with with sauce sauce.'"

Another reader took a poke at a company that advertises "red vin wine." In other words, red wine wine.

A bit more obscure, but still worthy, is this one from Robert R. Cook: "How about 'NIC card'? Network Interface Card card."

Another Cook favorite does not qualify as a redundancy but is absolutely irresistible. He sent a cell-phone photo he took at the Royal Buffet behind Chapel Hill Mall showing this sign posted at the buffet line: "Please Do Not Laid the Whole Tongue on the Food."

Yes, that would be in extremely bad taste. Whatever it means.

MORE WORD FUN

A fellow who identifies himself only as "a faithful reader" wrote: "My wife and I were traveling recently. Her entree arrived and it had not been cooked the way she had asked. The server asked if my wife would like the meat to be 'upcooked.'

"Yes, the temptation was too great: I did ask what they would do to 'downcook' a piece of meat."

FLEETING FAME

Lee Friend of Cuyahoga Falls was getting her garage door repaired last week when the news broke that Elizabeth Taylor had died. After hearing about it on TV, she went to check on the progress of the work.

After that discussion, she passed along the news about Liz to the repairman, a fellow who appeared to be in his 40s.

His response: "'Oh.' Pause. "Is she from here?"

March 29, 2011

Poor Use of Language Irks Readers

I didn't realize so many people care about the language. A recent column about mangled phrases drew a slew of additional nominations.

WASTED WORD

Bob: I'm enjoying your word peeves as you report them. Here's one that bugs me. Why do so many people, especially TV news and weather reporters, always say, "and also"? Those words are synonyms and shouldn't be used together.

Mark Miller, Plain Township

Mark: Didn't your mother warn you about watching too much television?

WHERE'D THEY GO?

Bob: The one I don't understand is: Someone has "gone missing." Does it mean they are missing because they are gone, or gone because they are missing? Why aren't they just missing?

I don't wish to belabor the point, but if a person is gone, that is pretty definite. They're gone—period. But if they are missing, they might be found. So using both of them together says it could be one or the other. I don't think so.

Ruth Hale, Akron

Ruth: But what if they're gone and you're missing them?

EXTRA CHEAP

   Bob: The one I like is "free gift."

                              Allan Robinson, Wadsworth

Allan: Either way, the price is right.

APPETITE KILLER

   Bob: When did the word "starved" become an adjective? "Starved" is the past tense of the verb "starve." I often hear someone say, "I am starved," which is grammatically incorrect. Since "am" is a verb, it must be modified by an adverb (starving), not a verb used as an adjective. The correct use of "starved" is, "The dog starved to death because he was starving." I have also seen the incorrect use of "starved" in novels and in newspaper articles. Yikes!

   Was there an English grammar change of which I was not notified?

                              Merry Holmes, Akron

Merry: I don't know, but I just lost my appetite.

DIRECTIONALLY CHALLENGED

   Bob: One of my pet peeves is: "Are you coming with?" Coming with what, who, us, me?

   Is this phrase a product of too much tweeting or texting? My wife and I are trying to break our 7-year-old grandson of this, but I suspect it's a lost cause.

   Miss Leach, my high school English teacher, would come back from the grave and smack us on the back of the head with the ruler she carried as her deterrent to mucking up the English language!

   She is also responsible for me still remembering part of Samuel Taylor Coleridge's Rime of the Ancient Mariner, Part II, and Marc Antony's funeral oration from Shakespeare's Julius Caesar.

                              Ken Roskos, Green

Ken: You remember only part of those lessons? There's a ruler-toting ghost in your future.

MISPLACED PRIORITIES

Bob: I was an English teacher for many years. When my students would say, "Me and my friend . . ." I would correct them and tell them that you always place yourself last. You don't want to indicate that you are more important than the other person!

I would also ask them to say the sentence again and take the other person's name out.

When they would say, "Me [did something]," they would realize that they had used the incorrect pronoun.

You can excuse a small child for using "me" because their world revolves around themselves, but as we grow older we should expect more.

Jerry Lichty, Wadsworth

Jerry: Actually, I *still* believe the world revolves around me. But at least I know better than to say it out loud.

Sept. 20, 2011

Readers Are Feeling Pet Peevish

Had I known you folks were harboring so many language peeves, I would have raised the topic years ago and saved myself a lot of work.

You now have given me enough pet peeves to keep me in columns through 2021.

Enter this fray at your own risk, though, because we have discovered that the "people in glass houses" syndrome definitely applies here.

A reader who last week claimed the sentence "I am starved" is grammatically incorrect was pounced on by four readers. Here's one:

She states that "starved" is the past tense of the verb "starve." However, "starved" is also the past participle of that verb, and past participles are used as adjectives all of the time. It is no different from saying, "The door is closed" or "My arm is broken." She also suggests that the word "starving" is an adverb. In fact, it is a participle or a gerund, depending on its usage, but not an adverb.

Alan G. Segedy, Akron

Alan: Congratulations on getting the word "gerund" into my column. That's a first. I hope it's a last. "Gerund" sounds like some sort of unpleasant medical condition.

ZIP FOR TWO

Bob: The man from Green, in mentioning his pet peeves, wrote: "She is also responsible for ME STILL remembering. . . ."

My high school English teacher, Elizabeth Graham, would have used her red pencil on that sentence. She taught that a possessive must be used before a participle—in other words, "my remembering."

Also, I believe the word "still" is redundant. If you are remembering now, you still remember.

Miriam Hall, Canton

Miriam: Fuggedaboutit.

PHRASE IS MIA

Bob: What happened to "to be," as in, "The lawn needs mowed"?

Herman Bennett, Barberton

Herman: As best I can tell, those words were taken captive by people from Pittsburgh and Youngstown and haven't been seen since.

FEWER BRAINS

Bob: How about this one from a Mercedes Benz commercial? "More styling, more power, LESS doors!"

Al Risaliti, Jackson Township

Al: I first saw that spot on *Monday Night Football*. I assumed the person who wrote it suffered one too many helmet-to-helmet hits.

IN THE CLEAR

Bob: Please advise as to whether I am justified to exercise my pet: "try and make," as in, "It didn't seem feasible to try and make the flight." Isn't it "try to make," or am I the errant one?

Jan Wenrick, Stow

Jan: I can't vouch for your overall lack of errancy, but you seem to be error-free in this regard. Good luck rebooking your flight.

EVIL TREND

Bob: One of the Ohio-isms I've been noticing lately is the rise of the dreaded triple-possessive.

Specifically: your guys's (pronounced: yer GUY-zizz). As in, "Are those your guys's coats?" I thought it must've been a mistake the first time I heard it, but I've heard it at least half-a-dozen times in the last year.

Jim McIntyre, Cuyahoga Falls

Jim: Youse right, and all them guyses is wrong.

SEEING SOMETHING

Bob: My own pet peeve is the substitution of subject pronouns for object pronouns, found especially after prepositions and the conjunction "and." For example, "He was seen by her and I." Remove the "her and" and most people would see the error, "He was seen by I."

Robert Gaebel, New Franklin

Robert: Unless you were Sgt. Schultz, in which case you'd see nothing.

DOUBLING DOWN

Bob: I have been reading the pet peeves that people submit, but I haven't seen mine. It is the redundant expression "exact same." I guess people think it sounds great because I have seen and heard it used in TV commercials, heard commentators use it and read it in novels. That is like saying "same same." You would think that ad writers and people who write speeches would have a better knowledge of grammar.

Doris Troyer, Canal Fulton

Doris: You'll like the next writer, because he's saying precisely the exact same similar thing. Plus more.

KID STUFF

Bob: "Same exact"—you might as well say "red red." Or when our local weather people say, "The white stuff is coming." Say the word "snow." "White stuff" makes you sound as if you are 5 years old.

Ken Boughton, North Canton

Ken: Either that or it sounds as if you're expecting a shipment from Colombia.

Sept. 27, 2011

Language Quirkiness Still Runs Rampant

We've created a monster.

Submissions continue to roll in from people who can't wait to get a pet language peeve off their chest.

As we sort through these, though, we might be well-advised to keep this matter in perspective.

Recently I was a guest on WCPN (90.3-FM), the NPR station in Cleveland. One of the other guests was John McWhorter, a noted linguist and author whose books include *Doing Our Own Thing: The Degradation of Language and Music and Why We Should, Like, Care.*

To him, that degradation is a double-edged sword. A loosening of proper language makes the society "less elitist," he says, because people aren't instantly judged by their command of the language— or lack thereof.

The flip side, though, is that it also makes us "less reflective." If we don't structure our language with care, especially the written language, we lose the ability to convey nuances and complex thoughts.

But, as McWhoter noted, if language never changed at all, you and I would be speaking in the style of *Beowulf.*

In which case . . . shoot me in the head.

MISSING WORD

Bob: Let me join in the fun. My pet peeve is, "I seen it," and variations thereof. What ever happened to the word "saw"?

Nancy Phelps, Randolph

Nancy: It looked in the mirror and saw "was." See the next item.

FOUND WORD

Bob: What ever happened to subjunctive mood and the prepositional phrase? "I wish I was dead." "If I was you, I'd ask for a raise." "I graduated college."

Dick Jacoby, Stow

Dick: Good point. The correct usage, of course, is, "I were graduated college."

HOME SCHOOLING

Bob: Why do we say, "I'm going to church," but we don't say, "I'm going to home"?

Bob Reymann, Akron

Bob: I'm not sure, but readers frequently tell me I should be sent "to a home."

HEALTH MATTERS

Bob: My suggestion is the correction of the use of the word "healthy." Being healthy is a state of being in good health. Foods are not healthy; they assist in keeping a person in good health.

Therefore, "healthy recipes," "healthy exercise," etc., are misnomers. The correct word is "healthful."

Elinor Brown, Rittman

Elinor: I personally think it's unhealthy to use the words "et cetera." But if you ever say them aloud, please do so correctly. If you don't, you'll have to answer to the next reader.

SILVER TONGUE

Marv Strach of Silver Lake hates when people pronounce "et cetera" as "ECK cetera."

I'll add a couple of my own pronunciation peeves:

"Nuclear" is "NUKE-lee-er," not "NUKE-you-ler."

And coupon is "COO-pon," not "CUE-pon."

WALK THIS WAY

Bob: It is "walk the talk" and not "walk the walk" or "talk the talk." "Walk the talk" is an AA slogan for getting people to act on their verbalizations (aka put your money where your mouth is).

David Culp, Akron

David: If it were simply "talk the talk," life would be a lot easier, eh?

HALF A RECIPE

An Akron letter writer who prefers anonymity offered several contributions, among them a peeve I share: A "cement" walkway or patio is in fact "concrete." Cement is only one ingredient in concrete.

NO, HE WON'T

Bob Dove of Cuyahoga Falls hates when people say, "If you will," attempting to sound sophisticated.

EMPTY WORDS

A fellow who left a message but not a last name chastised "the media" for saying "oh" when they should be saying "zero." If you ask me, somebody who lumps all the media together and then won't leave his name deserves a score of zero.

Oct. 11, 2011

Grating On Their Ears

As readers continue to flood my email bag with their pet language peeves, more and more folks are beefing about pronunciation.

(Has the word "beef" become a legitimate verb?)

BAD BLEND

Bob: Listen to WNIR, WKSU or just about any radio station that broadcasts speech. For some reason, a lot of folks have a lazy mouth when it comes to the word "years." It comes out as "THISH SHEARS event."

It is not everyone, but a fair amount of them, even on NPR, which one would think would be more careful about pronunciation.

Yes, I know that there are more pressing problems in the world, but it just grates on the ears.

Elias Vujovich, Southington

Elias: You seem to be implying that WNIR would not grate on the ears if its hosts pronounced their words more clearly. Don't be silly.

STANDING ROOM ONLY

Bob: It's amazing to me that people continue to say "am-PHL-itheater" rather than "am-PHI-theater."

Ted Curtis, VP, University of Akron

Ted: I agree. That's a funny way to pronounce "Blossom."

IN THE KNOW

Bob: Speaking of pet peeves, one of mine is "pitcher" for "picture." Do people not know the difference?

Also, no one should be allowed to speak on radio or TV if they cannot complete a sentence without a "you know" or two (or more). Including you, Mr. D. (I watch NewsNite *Akron.)*

Y. Grace Porter, Akron

Grace: I have appeared on *NewsNite* exactly once, in September. You're branding me as a perpetual you-knower based on one appearance?

Horrified by your missive, I went online, clicked on the archived show and kept score. And I'm here to tell you that your favorite columnist unleashed only eight "you knows" in a half-hour of conversation. By contrast, fellow guests Phil Trexler and Jody Miller dropped 25 and 15, respectively.

So I'm, like, way more polished, and should definitely have my own show.

WRONG ROAD

Bob: This word-abuse is usually committed by TV news personalities: berry vs. bury.

"John Smith died yesterday and will be 'berried' (strawberry or blueberry?) on Saturday." Makes me so crazy I want to berry my head in a bowl of "razzberries," but that's another issue.

Alice Deffibaugh, Bath

Alice: This will make you even crazier: My *Webster's New World College Dictionary* confirms what I thought: Both words are pronounced exactly the same.

Now, if you're talking about the word "burry," meaning full of burs, then you're right. Otherwise, you'd better bury that peeve immediately.

At least you had the guts to use your name. Not so with a letter writer who was all fired up because he or she thinks broadcasters are erroneously interchanging the pronunciations of "your" and "you're."

"You are" as a contraction cannot be pronounced "your." They are two different words.

Yes, they are two different words, sir or madam, but in all my years on the planet, I've never heard anyone attempt to draw a distinction between their pronunciations.

That's because there isn't one. As my Webster's puts it, both are pronounced "yoor."

BAD AFTERTASTE

Bob: An irritant is when people order bruschetta from the menu and call it "BRUSH-etta," when it should be pronounced "BRUSK-eta." I always want to ask them if they pronounce zucchini as "ZUSH-inni" or Chianti as "SHEE-anti." This mispronunciation is most often committed by staff at some of our local so-called Italian restaurants.

David Culp, Akron

David: Fair warning: If you ask the wrong person about mispronouncing Chianti, you could end up with red stains on your shirt. And not just from the wine.

PLENTY OF PETS

Bob: If you're still on the subject, I'll add mine:
- *Sherbet is not "sherbert."*
- *Height is not "heighth."*
- *Aerate is not "air-ee-ate."*
- *The folks in Green need to pronounce Boettler Road correctly. It's "BET-ler, not BOT-ler."*

Nancy Sauer, Akron

Nancy: Correct. And I'll bet members of the Boettler family would like to aerate the folks who want to bottle them.

Oct. 20, 2011

Word Woes Still Driving Them Mad

If you guys would quit doing that, I'd quit doing this.

You: sending in all those pet language peeves. Me: printing them.

Oops—sorry for referring to you collectively as "guys," which I tend to do. That offends at least one of my female readers, who notes, "Last time I checked, I was a gal."

BAD KIDS

Bob: *You deserve an "A" for pointing out our incorrect pronunciations and misuse of words.*

Here's mine: Raise vegetables, not children. Children should be reared—or praised, admonished, punished or disowned, as the parent(s) deem necessary.

Edwina Wagner, Norton

Edwina: You are exactly right. Kids should be praised, admonished, punished and disowned, and only then forced to eat vegetables.

NOT SO GOLDEN

Bob: *There seems to be a trend both in the general populous as well as emergency dispatchers to give the location of the Golden Arches as "Mac Donald's" rather than McDonald's.*

Greg Santos, Canal Fulton

Greg: If emergency dispatchers are making that many references to McDonald's, McDonald's has bigger problems than pronunciation.

LOTS MORE-ER

Bob: *When, where and why did everyone start adding "more" when an "-er" does just fine?*

Examples: more friendly, more dirty, more calm. Whatever hap-

pened to friendlier, dirtier, calmer? People adding "more" is like chalk on a blackboard to my ears.

Peggy Heh, Hudson

Peggy: Then take your ears off the blackboard!

WRONG TEMP

Bob: Why do people take things out of the freezers to "unthaw" them? Aren't they doing the opposite?

Dan from Kenmore

Dan: I don't know, but your last name must have melted.

COMIC RELIEF

Bob: My mispronunciation pet peeve is how people continually mis-pronounce "Whadda ya' gonna do?" as "What are you going to do?" It's so pretentious!

Alan G. Segedy, Akron

Alan: That's too funny. Seriously. Quit upstaging me.

BLAST FROM PAST

Tim Hayes, a retired Beacon Journal copy editor, approached with a gleam in his eye.

"It's nice to see we have solved all of the world's problems," he said.

Huh?

"Everybody has 'issues' today. Nobody has 'problems.' "

DOUBLE DISAPPOINTMENT

Bob: If you're still accepting language pet peeves, I have a couple for your consideration:

1. Adding extra syllables to words. Athlete is a two-syllable word. It is not ATH-THE-LETE. That sounds like a second-grader sounding out a new word.

2. I know it is painful to watch the Cleveland Browns, but one televi-

sion commentator refers to the Cleveland offense as "ow"fense.

I shudder every time I hear these.

Charles E Hoover Jr., Uniontown

Charles: I shudder every time I hear the phrase "Cleveland Browns' offense," because clearly it does not employ enough top-flight ATH-THE-LETES. Thirteen years after coming back and they still can't move the ball.

BUCK STOPS HERE

Bob: I enjoyed your articles regarding grammar. You might have mentioned our president's "dumbing down" of the English language. He replaces the word "going" with "gonna." He also drops the "g" off words that end in "-ing." If our leaders are asking us to follow their examples, then let them lead with professionalism and the best they have to offer.

Lynn Miller, Akron

Lynn: Oh, how I wish sloppy articulation were our leaders' biggest problem.

'R' BEFORE 'E'

Bob: A day doesn't pass that I do not hear about someone who will: "pervide" information, "perduce" and "permote" shows, "pertect" animals and then "ferget" to feed them, "perdict" the next storm and "perject" the damage, or "perticipate" in activities."

Ken Preston, Akron

Ken: Thanks for helping to perduce my column.

Nov. 1, 2001

THE BIGGER PICTURE

Springfield, Highland Personify School Extremes

Highland High School is about six miles from the Akron city limits.

Springfield High School is about two.

In remedial math, they'd tell you that's a difference of four miles. Actually, it's a lot more.

The distance between Highland High and Springfield High is life-altering.

Northwest of Akron, in the heart of Medina County's Granger Township, Highland boasts a gorgeous, $37 million school that opened in 2003.

It looks more like a small private college. A winding driveway leads through beautifully landscaped grounds to a sprawling building that is open and airy, with skylights and huge windows. Each day, shiny buses deliver the students to classrooms that offer every modern convenience.

Now venture southeast of Akron, just past Wayside Furniture on Canton Road.

Part of Springfield's high school was built in 1931. That would be the part with classrooms that feature brown plastic wastebaskets lined up on window sills, ready to catch the water that flows in every time it rains.

Sometimes, the wastebaskets aren't enough. Last week, several computer keyboards got soaked.

There's a big, ugly, plastic awning above the sidewalk leading to the "new" part of the school that directs rainwater away from the foundation.

Walk the dank lower hallway and you can smell the mold. A student with asthma was such a wreck after his first day that he now gets home instruction.

Although Springfield has multiple students in wheelchairs, one

building isn't handicap-accessible and the other is only if the elevator is working, which it isn't.

In mid-tour, the principal cautions a visitor to be careful lest he
trip down a stairwell in a main hallway where a big chunk of tread
is missing.

The door to the old gym sticks so badly that the visitor needs to
help the principal yank it open. That gym isn't used much anymore
because large clumps of material occasionally fall from the ceiling.

The buses? Well, there aren't many. About 1,000 Springfield kids
have been without rides for a year.

Principal Cynthia Frola tries to walk an impossible tightrope
between not damaging school morale and communicating just how
bad things can get when a district defeats five levies in two years in
a state where the educational funding system has repeatedly been
ruled unconstitutional but nobody seems to do anything about it.

She says she fears test scores may soon plummet because of mandated cuts in the number of classes and because "we've lost the
cream of the crop" to private schools.

"We still have very capable students here," she says. "I don't want
to say anything negative, because I love these kids to death. But it's
tough."

The situation isn't much better at the elementary schools. To the
east, at Roosevelt, the bright red bricks of 1931 have turned dark red
and are now accented by hundreds of feet of gray caulk snaking its
way across the front, attempting to seal the cracks of 76 years' worth
of freezing, thawing and settling.

On the third floor of the old section, water drips in above the
windows whenever it rains.

Average age of Springfield's school buildings: 67 years.

Now, you don't need to study in a Taj Mahal to get a good education. But you ought to be able to keep the rain out and the ceilings
intact and the mold at bay.

How can we consistently turn our backs on kids whose only sin
was being born to parents who live in places like Springfield Township rather than places like Granger Township?

It is one of the great embarrassments of our age.

Sept. 6, 2007

Akrons, Akrons Everywhere

Akron, Ohio, has an inferiority complex.

Try as we might to deny it, most of us would have to admit under oath that we're a bit intimidated by the hulking city of Cleveland just 29 miles to our north.

And most of us would confess to being irked that nobody outside Ohio seems to know anything about us. Say the word "Akron" and you get one of two responses: a blank stare or a dated comment about rubber.

Well, if you think *we've* got problems, you ought to see our offspring. They're a mess.

Our city has spawned no fewer than 12 little Akrons. They're spread all over the continental United States, from Michigan to Alabama, from Pennsylvania to Colorado. And the biggest has a population of only 4,046.

As if that weren't bad enough, some of our children have turned into ingrates. They know absolutely nothing about their roots—and, in some cases, don't even seem to care.

We figured it was high time for a family meeting. To that end, we visited every one of the little Akrons.

Spent 21 days on the road.

Traveled 9,400 miles.

Stayed at 16 motels.

Drove eight rental cars.

Took 22 airplane flights.

And, yes, the sobs you hear are coming from the Beacon Journal's finance department.

But, starting Sunday, you can meet all the little Akrons. A different town will be featured on each of 12 consecutive days.

In laying out our reunion plans, we established one key ground rule: Every Akron had to be a specific dot on the map. If the name applied only to a township, it didn't count. There had to be a *there* there.

Still, we found Akrons, Akrons everywhere. In Alabama. Colorado. Iowa. Illinois. Indiana. Kansas. Michigan. Missouri. Mississippi. Nebraska. New York. Pennsylvania.

Alas, repeated attempts to find one in Hawaii proved unsuccessful.

Had we included townships, we would have added a trip to Minnesota, because that state has two, one in Big Stone County, right next to South Dakota, and the other in Wilkin County, 50 miles north.

At least one former Akron is now defunct. Akron, Ark., has gone the way of Atlantis.

The portability of our name seems odd, given that hardly anybody knows what it means.

Let's get this straight once and for all: The name Akron was derived from an ancient Greek word, *acros*, which meant high.

The choice seemed appropriate when our city was born in 1825, because Akron was the highest point on the Ohio & Erie Canal, which ran all the way from Lake Erie to the Ohio River.

The canal was our reason to be. Our city grew up around it and because of it.

But in March 1913, with the ground covered with snow, we got 10 inches of rain in three days. Trying to ease massive flooding, we blew up the locks, essentially wiping out the canal.

The state decided not to rebuild because of the cost and the fact that the railroads were taking over as the main form of transportation.

In fact, the railroads were the key to spreading Akron's name. As the Iron Horse carted more and more people westward, they took the name with them. Many of the early rail lines ran precisely east and west, which is why five of the little Akrons are within one degree of our latitude.

A lot of the new Akrons were settled by people from Medina County. But remember: Until 1840, there was no such thing as Summit County. Akron was in Portage County, and Medina County was right next door. It included Copley, Bath, Richfield and Norton.

The "other" Akrons don't offer a lot of demographic diversity. With the exception of Akron, Ala.—where 81 percent of the population is African-American—our offspring are overwhelmingly white, overwhelmingly older than the national median age, and largely Republican.

We went into each place cold. In other words, we didn't call ahead to set up interviews. We wanted to focus on first impressions. We also didn't want to give people a chance to bone up on our Akron.

One of the biggest surprises during our journey was discovering that our Akron has a resource many other places would kill for: an abundance of water.

Sure, we have squabbles about who gets access to various supplies and for how much. But Northeast Ohio is wonderfully wet. Dick Celeste had it right as Ohio's governor when he declared, way back in the 1980s, that we should be known not as the "Rust Belt" but as the "Water Belt." In many of the other Akrons, the water is too salty, too polluted or too far beneath the surface, or there's just not enough of it.

The little Akrons haven't missed the chance to play around with our good name. Someone in Colorado reversed the letters and opened a Norka Restaurant. Iowa has a Norka Street. Pennsylvania has a Norka Christmas Tree Farm.

In our Akron, of course, the reverse spelling is most closely identified with Norka Futon. (Newcomers are excused for being puzzled not only by the word "Norka" but also by "futon," which is a type of bed.)

We also discovered that, in the world of journalism, there's no such thing as an original idea.

In Akron, Ind., an 80-year-old woman named Velma Bright surprised us by saying she was familiar with the Beacon Journal. She remembered talking to a reporter in "the late '40s or early '50s." She even remembered the name: Fran Murphey.

Apparently, the late Beacon Journal legend was roaming around on one of her countless field trips and showed up in Indiana unannounced. Dogged reporter that she was, Fran asked to be directed to the home of the person who had the best handle on the town's history. She was sent to Velma's house.

Velma wasn't home. So Fran took a picture of her car in front of the house and later mailed the photo to Velma.

Fran's story is still in our archives. It was written in 1951.

The bad news: After all these years, hardly anyone else in the other Akrons seems to know a single thing about our Akron.

Wouldn't you think people living in a place called Akron would have a passing familiarity with a city of the same name that has a population of a quarter-million? But no.

Almost everyone we encountered was, however, amused by our quest. In Akron, Iowa, where two weekly newspapers are battling over a total circulation of about 2,000, a Beacon Journal writer and photographer were turned into celebrities. People from both papers took our picture and wrote a story about our visit. (Talk about a slow news day.)

Our journey to all things Akron also triggered a new appreciation for the sheer size of this country. An incredible amount of land is sitting out there, the vast majority of it vacant.

Residents of our Akron sometimes refer to their home as either the smallest big city in America or the biggest small town. We forget how many people live in areas so sparsely populated that they consider ours to be a megalopolis.

Lump together the total population of the 12 other Akrons, and you get 12,486 people.

That's not even 6 percent of our population. Heck, that's 975 fewer people than live in Copley Township.

But the story of the other Akrons is less about numbers than people—unique people with unique, often fascinating histories. Like many residents of our Akron, they are the descendants of hearty souls who were trying to carve out a bustling, prosperous community from scratch.

Most of them failed—if you judge simply by population figures. But in many important senses, most of them succeeded. These people like their Akrons. They like their neighbors. They like their lives. And they like the fact that they are part of the fabric of the unprecedented success story known as the United States.

In a 1949 book celebrating the centennial of Akron, N.Y., an author expressed a sentiment still shared by many in small-town America: "Akron stands today at the threshold of another century, a village among thousands of other villages that comprise this great country—villages founded of families of free people who had the courage to rise, with God's help, and build a nation today unequalled in strength and wealth and freedom."

Our trek spurred a renewed appreciation for the United States— not necessarily for its government, but for the people who populate it.

It is the people we'll remember, the many, many people who were open and inquisitive and willing to meet a total stranger halfway. People who treasure their history, who work hard, who do the right thing—even when no one is watching. They are people, we'd like to think, just like us.

Nov. 22, 2003

Tiny Rules Add Up to a Big Pain

It wasn't the last straw. I'm sure there are many more straws to come.

But for some reason, it was particularly discouraging.

Perhaps it was a reminder of the sheer volume of these changes. Pile them up, year after year, and eventually you look around and see a different world than the one you saw just a decade earlier.

What set me off was a sign taped to the door of my bank: "Please remove sunglasses, hats and hoods."

I had never seen a sign like that, but I immediately knew why it had been posted: Removing my shades and cap would make it easier for the cops to identify me on a surveillance video if I tried to rob the place.

I wasn't going to try to rob the place. Heck, I haven't thought seriously about robbing a bank since the first time I watched *Butch Cassidy and the Sundance Kid.*

And I would estimate that 99.995 percent of the people who walk through the door of my bank have no plans for a stickup, either. So yet again, 0.005 percent of the population has changed daily life for all of the rest of us.

Is removing your hat and sunglasses a major imposition? No. It's trivial. But this is one more order to "toe the line" directed at people who already toe the line.

Not too many years ago, we could roll into a gas station, fill up the tank, walk inside and hand over the correct amount of cash. No more. You must either use a credit card or guess how much gasoline your tank will hold. And if you guess wrong, you have to go back inside to retrieve your excess cash.

In other words, you have to "prepay in advance," as the stickers read, with laughable redundancy, on a number of area gas pumps.

When you go to the airport, you have to remove your shoes. Why? Because one whack job tried to create a shoe bomb. Had he tried to sneak on a nose bomb, we'd probably all have to blow our noses on a hanky before passing through security.

To make matters worse, we're adamant about being politically correct. We wand little old ladies in wheelchairs who wouldn't dream about trying to take down a plane in a billion years.

Why? Because we're being "fair." Never mind that not one little old lady has attempted to take down an airliner in the history of aviation.

That's not fairness; that's stupidity—a waste of time and resources and an insult to our intelligence.

When we go to a basketball game at the Q and pay an obscene amount of money at the concession stand for a bottle of water, the person who collects our cash now twists off the little plastic cap and retains it, apparently so we're not tempted to fling it onto the court.

Never mind that a full bottle of water would be much more damaging. Never mind that, without a cap, we are far more likely to accidentally dump our water on a fellow spectator. We all go capless because somebody sat in some meeting and decided this was sound policy.

I'm tired of my life changing because of the bad guys. I'm tired of being guilty until proven innocent.

And now that we're warmed up, here's the other end of the importance spectrum.

Not too many years ago, you could drive down the road and, if you weren't doing anything wrong, you'd be left alone. You were presumed to be a law-abiding citizen and a safe driver unless you displayed evidence to the contrary.

No more. In 2010, you can be minding your own business and suddenly be detained and forced to prove your innocence at a "sobriety checkpoint." *Show me your papers, comrade, and let me smell your breath.*

This matter is far from trivial. This is a sea change in the way Americans live their lives. This is how things are done in totalitarian countries.

Yes, I've written about this several times before. And every time I do, a bunch of readers accuse me of advocating drunken driving. Most of the rest of them simply shrug.

Half the nation is raising holy hell over the Arizona law that requires immigrants to carry documents and gives authorities the power to detain them if they suspect they're here illegally. A Catholic cardinal in Los Angeles said the practice is akin to "Nazism." How is that one iota worse than allowing authorities to demand the documents of a person who just happens to be driving down a certain road at a certain hour?

Societies don't change overnight. They change almost imperceptibly, like a coastline slowly reshaped by the seemingly harmless lapping of waves. Societies change not only with the big breakers—"Show us your papers"—but also with the tiniest of swells—"Please remove you sunglasses."

One day you look around—with or without your shades—and you no longer recognize the place.

July 8, 2010

Our Colors Might Clash for Eternity

When I was a senior in high school, right on the brink of graduation, my father's best friend asked me a question at a dinner party.

"What do you consider to be the most serious problem facing the country?"

I still remember the question, because it seemed odd in that setting. In my family, much like Beaver Cleaver's, dinner-table conversation usually centered around less gritty, more personal topics.

For that same reason, I still remember my answer. After weighing a handful of possible responses, I said: "Race relations."

Only a few years before that, race riots had erupted in the Hough area of Cleveland and, later, in Glenville, a couple of miles from my father's workplace. MLK had been assassinated. Tommie Smith and John Carlos had made their black-gloved stand at the Olympics. Race was red-hot, and seemed to influence and overshadow almost everything else—perhaps even the Vietnam War.

That question was posed to me 39 years ago. Today, I'm not certain I wouldn't give exactly the same answer.

Nearly four decades later, after all of the marches and the rallies and the speeches and the anti-discrimination laws and affirmative action and diversity training and Rodney King and "Coming Together" and "Town Hall meetings" and the election of a president of color by a white majority . . . despite all of that and much, much more, this country, in some ways, hasn't changed a bit.

Racial tension continues to lurk an inch below the surface. People of all shades continue to suspect race is a motive even in situations where race has absolutely nothing to do with it.

My latest personal example: Tiger Woods.

Yeah, I know. You're tired of hearing about him—allegedly. But the networks, newspapers and websites wouldn't have stayed on the subject for six weeks if the public weren't still devouring every syllable.

Last month, immediately after the revelations that he apparently had slept in every fourth bed in America, I wrote a tongue-in-cheek column in which I asked several women in Akron—where Tiger collectively has spent two months of his adulthood—whether they ever helped him "celebrate."

That night, at 11:40 p.m., a man with a scratchy monotone left a barely discernable message on my voice mail. He judged the column "very distasteful"—and knew my motive for writing it.

"I see you as a white imperial, probably of some Eastern descent, so it's almost in your bloodline that when a person of any type of color has any allegations of doing something, [you want to] make them look bad."

The caller didn't leave a name or number—big surprise—so I wasn't able to tell him that my heritage is mainly Scottish and German, with one branch dating back to the American Revolution.

Or maybe he was talking about the Eastern United States. Not really sure. If so, he was wrong on that count, too.

Of course, the man wasn't really looking for dialogue. He was reveling in his anonymity.

"I just wanted to tell you that I thought the article was the biggest load of crap I've ever read. And it seems like your dream job would be to get out of the little Akron Beacon Journal and to end up on Fox News."

Or maybe NBC News, which, two days after my column, broadcast an hourlong *Dateline* consisting solely of the Tiger Woods controversy.

Does any rational person think NBC did that because Tiger is a person of color?

Or maybe, just maybe, NBC was thinking what I was thinking: Tiger Woods is one of the two or three most famous people on the face of the planet.

Here we had a young billionaire, a guy with unprecedented sports success, international fan worship, a gold-plated lifestyle and a cover-girl wife.

Lest we forget, the media gave full-throttle coverage—and endless late-night ridicule—to Bill/Monica and Letterman/interns. In fact, those lily-white trysts received so much coverage that I can print the names with no need for further explanation.

In Tiger's case, rarely is a man *less* closely identified with a single race. He has proudly identified himself as "Caublanasian." If anyone is color-neutral, it's Tiger. If he were a wall in your house, he wouldn't even be beige; he'd be a window.

No matter. I had made fun of a person with some coloring, so I was a "white imperial."

The day after that phone call, I was listening to rapper Snoop Dogg on Howard Stern's satellite radio show. (Say what you will about Howard, but no other interviewer on radio or television is able to consistently draw more information out of celebrity guests.)

During a fascinating and otherwise rational conversation, Snoop Dogg unleashed a conspiracy theory: Much of the money behind Obama's victory came from the Ku Klux Klan.

I smiled, thinking he was setting up a punch line. Unfortunately, he wasn't. In his mind, the last election went something like this:

The KKK hates black people, and the KKK knew that the next president would be Inheriting horrible problems. If Obama were that next president, he would have no chance of fixing the problems quickly, which would cause white people to blame him and give Whitey an even bigger reason to hate blacks and maybe start a race war.

Say *what?*

This from a guy who is worth in the neighborhood of $100 million (much of it coming from white folks).

I was reminded of all of this Monday morning, my first day back at work after two weeks off, when I opened an e-mail that began:

"Dear Colleague:

"The American Anthropological Association is pleased to extend an invitation for you to attend 'A New National Dialogue on Race,' two days of programming designed to look at the racial issues that America faces in a brand new way."

To be held in Washington, D.C., it will consist of "symposia that examine how domestic policy initiatives, media coverage and the advocacy community can begin to shift current perceptions and misinformation about the concept of race."

Well, I wish them luck, but I'm going to pass.

I've been trying to figure this stuff out for more than 40 years, and I'm at a total loss. I am officially out of ideas. Fried.

As of today, I'm going on a racial hiatus. I'm not going to think about anything other than the most basic tenet of human interaction: trying to treat everyone the way I'd like to be treated unless a particular person gives me a reason to do otherwise.

When you can come up with something better, let me know.

Jan. 7, 2010

Goodwill's Trash is Her Treasure

She is standing in her cramped living room in the bowels of Nimmer Place, a public-housing complex for seniors on the eastern edge of Akron.

Even on this sunny summer afternoon, her basement apartment isn't getting much light.

Her hair and her sweatshirt are gray, and the paper bags and boxes in the center of the room are brown. But Marion Lesher's enthusiasm for her cause radiates from her face like a full-spectrum rainbow.

"Look at this one!" she exclaims, holding aloft a baby doll. "Isn't she precious?"

She unfurls a handsome oriental rug that appears to be unblemished.

"This is the kind of stuff they throw out all the time!"

By "they" she means the folks who run the Goodwill store at Midway Plaza.

For more than two years, Lesher has climbed into her electric wheelchair a couple of times a week and driven half a mile to Goodwill's Dumpsters, where she has used a garden tool to retrieve a wide variety of items she didn't think belonged in the trash.

Dolls. Rugs. Coffee makers. Baby blankets. Sleepers. Cooking pots. Decorations. Curling irons. Sweaters. Candles. Can openers. Purses. Shoes.

She brings them home, cleans and washes and tests them, putting new Energizers in the things that need batteries. Then her daughter swings by with a van, loads up everything and takes the items to the drop-off center at the Haven of Rest, a private shelter for the poor and homeless just east of downtown Akron.

"I must have 10 curling irons in mint condition," Lesher says, looking around the room. "Brought them home, plugged them in to see if they work. They're still in the box."

The concept of donating donations came to her one day while she was walking her dog at the plaza and noticed a Goodwill worker "throwing out good stuff."

"I got 12 grandchildren who don't want for nothing," says Lesher, 63, "but I know a lot of kids out there don't have that. . . . I know I'm making someone's kids happy, and that makes me happy."

She's not nearly as happy lately. Hasn't been since Aug. 25, when Goodwill e-mailed the Tallmadge Police Department to ask for assistance in shooing away garbage pickers.

Before Lesher began her mission in 2007, she called the Tallmadge police and asked whether it is illegal to take things from trash containers. She was told it was not.

"Many times when I was over there, I'd see the Tallmadge police circling around, and they'd say, 'Hey, are you getting anything good out of there?' I'd say, 'The Haven of Rest is gonna love me this week!' "

Tallmadge Police Lt. Ron Williams says garbage picking is not stealing, but, depending upon the circumstances, getting access to the container could be viewed as trespassing.

"I've driven behind that building many times and seen people in Dumpsters and let them go about their business because nobody cared at the time," says Williams. "In general, we don't ask people to leave Dumpsters unless we're requested by the management of the company—and in this case, we were."

Williams says Goodwill contacted the department after employees watched a man climb into the bed of his pickup truck and break the locks off of two Dumpsters, and in another case watched adults place children inside a Dumpster to do the scavenging.

Goodwill's Valerie Still, vice president for employee and public relations throughout a five-county region, says Goodwill has begun to lock Dumpsters primarily to prevent people from hurting themselves.

Even a woman in a wheelchair who is grabbing items with a garden tool?

"Even if she's got some sort of tool, the items in there could be broken or have some sort of sharp edges," says Still.

Well, OK. Maybe. But beyond that, why are all these apparently pristine items—some in their original boxes or with price tags still attached—going into the trash in the first place?

Still says "a large portion" of the nice-looking items are thrown out because they have been deemed dangerous by the Consumer Product Safety Commission. The remainder are "things that are broken that we couldn't salvage, or items like textiles, clothing that is mildewed or bug-infested."

When told Lesher washes, dries and sometimes even repackages clothing and bedding, she says, "We don't really have the capacity to wash or dry-clean any items, so if they are stained or mildewed or bug-infested, obviously we don't want to damage any other product on our store floor."

But the woman whose relatives call her the "Goodwill Bandit" insists Goodwill is fudging, that plenty of the discards are perfectly safe and desirable—especially to the homeless.

The Rev. Ben Walker, executive director of the Haven of Rest, says he doesn't know whether his group accepts things more readily because his items are handed out free, rather than sold. But he says the Haven has its own screening process, including a little workshop, that would catch anything dangerous. And the type of things Lesher has been donating are exactly what the Haven needs.

That's not always the case.

"We've had bowling balls donated," Walker says with a laugh. "What's a homeless person going to do with a bowling ball?"

The Haven doesn't particularly care where a donation comes from and doesn't ask.

"All I can say is, if the items she is dropping off are usable, and the things she's done work on are in good, usable order, then it has worked out well," says Walker.

Lesher isn't surprised her donations of donations are welcome at the Haven. But she is flabbergasted by Goodwill's stance.

"I'm not doing any harm," she says. "I'm not making a mess over there. I'm just a slightly soiled senior citizen trying to give things to people who can use them. . . .

"I was trying to do it incognito. I didn't want publicity. But when they told me they were going to arrest me if I go back over . . . "

I say throw the book at her. Just make sure it doesn't have any sharp edges.

Sept. 17, 2009

An Apple for the Teacher

You know the drill.

You're embarrassed to let people see you getting emotional. So instead of openly weeping—as every instinct in your body recommends—you stifle it. You give it the big-eye, no-blink, look-straight-ahead-and-pretend-nothing's-happening treatment. You figure that if a drip or two trickles down, you can simply take a quick, inconspicuous swipe, just like you do when you get a speck of dirt in your eye.

Nobody ever falls for it, of course. And the reason they don't fall for it is that most of them are doing exactly the same thing.

It happens in movie theaters. It happens at funerals. It usually doesn't happen in schools—at least not to parents. But that's exactly what happened the other day to a couple dozen moms and dads at an elementary school in suburban Akron.

One of the best teachers in the history of the world was hosting a year-end party for her kids and their parents. I'm not going to identify the teacher or the school. I don't want to embarrass her, and I don't want to make the future teachers of my children worry that anything they say or do might end up in the newspaper. But she knows who she is. The kids and parents know who she is. And if you've ever had a teacher like her, you, too, know exactly who she is.

She's someone who connects with her class on a personal level. Someone willing to go out on a limb. Someone willing to surrender a bit of the real estate in her comfort zone and make a genuine, loving commitment to children who are not her own.

Kids who are really, really lucky will get a handful of these teachers in their lifetime.

The parents had no trouble finding her classroom. They'd been there a lot during the previous nine months. The teacher had come up with dozens of excuses to get the moms and dads involved.

For this particular occasion, the youngsters put together a 40-minute video modeled after a morning television show, complete with news, sports, weather, traffic, gardening and cooking.

The writing and acting was done by the kids, and everyone had a speaking part.

Much of the video was unintentionally funny; much of it also showed remarkable creativity.

But the videotape that inflicted the tear-duct damage was a second, much shorter tape containing far less action.

This seven-minute presentation consisted of informal snapshots of the class taken throughout the year. Kids laughing. Kids on field trips. Kids with their arms around each other. Kids doing class projects. Kids mugging for the camera. Kids being kids—young, innocent, beautiful kids.

The soundtrack was strictly music. Sentimental stuff, like the old Bette Midler song, *Friends*.

On the surface, a videotape of still pictures is a contradiction in terms. But it was actually the perfect metaphor. The images were frozen, but only temporarily. The video rolled along like the river of time. A moment of joy. Dissolve. A moment of friendship. Dissolve. Another picture. Another scene. Already, another place and time. Another school year come and gone. Another year closer to depleting the innocence of the fresh-faced kids in the photos.

Innocence is an increasingly precious commodity these days. Kids have a hard time getting past third grade with much of it intact. And that explained some of the tears.

But these were also drips of joy. Parents were thinking about their great good fortune to have shared a time and place with an unassuming, middle-age woman for whom teaching is a job, a calling, a hobby and a passion.

On this particular morning, she seemed to be teaching the grownups. The lesson: Cherish what you have—in my case, a bright, funny, beautiful little girl who is living a great little-girl life.

I want to put the videotape on pause and leave it there. We all do. But we can't. We know that.

Sometimes we forget. Sometimes it takes a great teacher to remind us.

June 13, 1999

Vietnam Wall Works Best in the Rain

To a guy born in 1952, The Wall emits a siren song. The question is not *whether* it will get you. Only *when*.

The Wall jumped out and grabbed me Friday afternoon. I had just climbed into my car—fully expecting to drive home—when an unseen force took control of the steering wheel and delivered me to Triplett Boulevard on Akron's southeast side.

That's where a traveling replica of the Vietnam memorial has been luring visitors from all over the region since arriving last week.

I was prepared to get misty-eyed. I didn't.

I got mad. All over again.

Do you have any idea how big the number 58,209 is?

I didn't. Not really.

Sure, I knew it is bigger than the population of Cuyahoga Falls. I knew it is enough people to fill Jacobs Field and most of Gund Arena at the same time.

But until you see those names . . . all spelled out . . . all lined up . . . all real . . . all with a story . . . all from a family . . . you don't know how big 58,209 is.

I got mad because those 58,209 were not plucked from our neighborhoods by some foreign power. They were plucked by our own damn government. The biggest threat to our well-being was us.

I got mad at the men who let it happen, the bureaucratic twits like Robert McNamara, who finally admitted two years ago that he knew the war wasn't winnable long before most of those 58,209 qualified for a wall.

I got mad at the well-meaning American citizens who bought the lies. Mad that so many of them didn't think for themselves.

I got mad about all the vets who aren't on The Wall because they waited to die until they got home. Guys like my high school pal Craig, a good-natured, regular guy who dutifully trotted off to Vietnam and came home a lunatic, a midnight intruder who was justifiably killed by a terrified homeowner. Anyone who knew him knows Craig died from the same war.

I got mad about the people who belong on another sort of wall, a wall for the living dead.

Guys like Tim, a Wayne County resident who can no longer feel any emotion at all.

And I got mad about all the people like me who, because of Vietnam, can barely say the word "Washington" or "politics" without sneering—even though we realize cynicism isn't the solution.

This movable monument—60 percent as large as the permanent one—has certainly come to the right place. Middle America. Right beside a four-lane highway. Right across the street from a place whose sign identifies it as an "auto salvage" business—in plain English, a junkyard. We love to put fancy names on things to help obscure what those things really are.

In front of the junkyard is a billboard advertising Basic cigarettes It looms like a silent taunt, a reminder that we still live in a country that in some ways is fundamentally twisted. A country, for example, that subsidizes the growers of a product that kills us.

"Keep It Basic" reads the billboard.

Indeed.

I visited The Wall again yesterday. Friday's weather was too mild. I wanted to feel the rain.

Hundreds of others did, too. Tough-looking bikers in dripping black leather. Parents cooing at their infants. A woman in a fine Sunday dress walking around barefoot, mud up to her ankles. All of them feeling the rain.

Volunteers pulled apart bales of straw and scattered it in front of The Wall, hoping to cut down on the mud. But almost as soon as it was in place, footsteps pounded it into the earth, turning it wet and brown.

If you visit The Wall before it leaves on Thursday, you need to view it from both near and far.

First, get right up close and read the names. Lots and lots of names. Listen to their voices. The voices yelling, "Never again." Thank them for their message.

Then move back and sit on one of the benches. Let your gaze

become unfocused. Notice how the white letters on the black background are arranged so that, from a distance, the columns of names resemble tree trunks.

The problem, of course, was the opposite. The problem was the people who couldn't see the trees for the forest.

June 2, 1997

Your Show Won't Run Indefinitely

"The world erases us, little by little. The future is always
blooming in the slow decay of the past. The two meet in the
now."
— Bill O'Connor, Beacon Journal, March 1997

What a marvelous paragraph, buried deep in a story about an
Akron man watching the demolition of his former family home.

And what a great time of the year to trot it out again.

The last week of May always taps us on the shoulder and suggests
we stand back and examine how much of ourselves has been erased.

Although Memorial Day was created to honor war veterans, when
you hang around in cemeteries—as many of us did on Monday—you
can't help but be reminded that every living thing eventually stops
living.

That's a scary concept. It's one of the big-picture items that can
keep us awake at night, especially when we're young.

Kids tend to dwell on the big questions. To them, the questions
are newer. The lack of definitive answers is more troubling. Kids
haven't learned to push such matters into the background.

No wonder they're afraid of the dark. And no wonder the children's book *Goodnight Moon* is celebrating its 50th year in print.

In the great green room
There was a telephone
And a red balloon
And a picture of
The cow jumping over the moon.

The soothing mantras in this simple book have helped millions
of tiny tots fortify themselves against the awesome mysteries of the
cosmos.

But somewhere not far into adulthood, we begin to ignore those
gaping holes in our understanding. And by middle age, we have
become obsessed with the smallest of questions.

Should we weed-and-feed the lawn today or tomorrow? Can we get the garbage cans out soon enough to beat the pick-up? As if these sorts of things will matter a year from now.

Perhaps that's the only way we can continue to function. Perhaps staring directly at the big questions every day would burn out our retinas. Maybe the daily trivia is a fancy form of gallows humor.

We never really outgrow our fear of the dark, you know. We just manage to push it away for a while.

Toward the end of the road, in retirement, when the proverbial "slow decay of the past" begins to occupy our thoughts more than the potential bloom of the future, our focus swings back. No longer caught up in the day-to-day minutiae, we again find ourselves confronting the big question marks.

Researchers say people sleep less well as they cross into old age. Perhaps the reason is not as much physiological as psychological: Older folks know the end is approaching. And no matter how well prepared you are, no matter how strong your religion, surely there is at least a little piece of you that is apprehensive about death. Because nobody knows exactly what happens when you die. Nobody.

We ridicule the Hale-Bopp comet people, but do we know a whole lot more than they?

The point is not to drum up fear or depression or sacrilege, nor to suggest we should devote every waking hour to pondering our own mortality. But acknowledging it more often might give our lives more value.

Everybody knows life is fragile and finite. But for long periods of time we pretend it isn't.

If your life isn't working the way it should, or you're not happy with the way you've been acting, you need to fix it. Right away.

Based on recent statistics, about 5,000 Summit Countians who are alive today will be gone by Memorial Day 1998.

That might include you. It might include me.

The author of *Goodnight Moon* didn't make it to Memorial Day 1953. The illustrator didn't see Memorial Day 1989.

Neither you nor I know for sure how many Memorial Days we have left. But as of today, we both have one fewer.

Goodnight stars
Goodnight air
Goodnight noises everywhere.

Before you doze off tonight, take a moment to remind yourself that simply going through the motions isn't enough.

May 28, 1997

Black and White But Not Read All Over

At many area Walmarts, the book section is extremely well-organized.

The self-help books are here . . . the religion section is there . . . cooking and diet books farther down . . . and right over here is the black section.

You think I'm kidding?

At Walmart, apparently, skin color trumps all.

The "black section" contains everything written by and about blacks: romance novels, self-help books, religion, sports, even an autobiography by the current president of the United States.

Now, whether or not you're a fan of Barack Obama, can't we at least agree that the thing that defines him is not his skin color but his job title? We have lots and lots of African-Americans in this country—about 38 million, according to the U.S. Census Bureau—but during this country's entire 234-year history we have had only 43 presidents.

Yet there he is, right in the middle of six monochromatic shelves, peering out at us from the cover of *The Audacity of Hope.*

At the Walmart on Arlington Road in Springfield Township, you'll find two fancy hardcover books by people who are household names in professional football. Drew Brees, quarterback of the 2009 Super Bowl champion New Orleans Saints, smiles on the cover of *Coming Back Stronger: Unleashing the Hidden Power of Adversity.* Tony Dungy, coach of the 2006 Super Bowl champion Indianapolis Colts, smiles on the cover of *The Mentor Leader.*

But you won't find those books side by side. Why? Because Brees is white and Dungy is black.

The black guy goes in the black section. After all, who other than a black person would want to read a book by an insightful, ethical, inspirational football coach?

At the Walmart in Montrose, *Storm Warning,* by hugely popular white pastor Billy Graham, can be found in the religion section. But *Life Overflowing,* by hugely popular black pastor T.D. Jakes, is in the black section, along with Dungy and Obama and Sister Souljah and

Adrienne Byrd and all those other people whom Walmart believes are pretty much the same.

The positioning of books within the black shelves would be laughable if it weren't such a sorry commentary on Walmart's thought process—or lack thereof. For instance, directly beneath a faith book by gospel artist Kirk Franklin is a steamy novel called *The Hot Box,* whose back cover promises "fiery titillation."

The megachain's deep thinkers must have agonized over some of these decisions. Imagine the gnashing of teeth over Obama: Let's see . . . the guy is actually half-white, so maybe we should put him in the regular section . . . but he is also half-black, and people seem to regard him as the first black president . . . so I guess we should put him in the black section.

No doubt the placement of *To Kill a Mockingbird* presented a similar dilemma: Gosh . . . the plot revolves around a black man falsely accused of rape, and there are a bunch of black characters . . . but the book was written by a white woman, and most of the characters are white . . . so we'd better put this one in the section with the real novels.

Did the knuckleheads making these decisions give a moment's thought to anything beyond black and white? Hard to tell.

When asked why many of its stores have a "black section" that lumps together everyone from romance novelists to preachers to the president of the United States—even though they have little in common beside skin color—Wal-Mart Stores Inc. responded without really responding.

"The book sections in our stores are designed to meet customer demand and feedback at the local level," read an e-mail from Phillip Keene, a media-relations official at the company's headquarters in Bentonville, Ark.

"Like many national bookstores, and book sections at retailers across the country, some of our stores have a section for African-American-focused books, while a store in a different area of the country might have a large science-fiction section or Western section. . . .

"Additionally, our books are separated into hardcover bestsellers, paperback bestsellers and other categories and it's possible that titles could be moved to different areas of the book section based on demand or interest for that particular merchandise."

OK, then.

If I'm correctly reading between the lines, the one and only issue here is effective marketing, and Wal-Mart thinks that drawing distinct lines between white and black will add up to more green.

I doubt it. I think it's insulting and financially counterproductive.

Wal-Mart is doing nothing more than feeding one of this country's worst habits: looking at absolutely everything in black and white.

No one can dispute that skin color colors much of how we perceive things and how we are perceived. But not everything is black and white. And until we can get that through our collective heads, we have no chance of solving the race problem that has haunted this country for centuries and periodically threatens to tear it apart.

Sept. 2, 2010

Life Stories No Longer Seem So Long

Drove through my ol' hometown the other day.

Past the old elementary school, which is no longer a school.

Past the old high school baseball field, which is no longer the high school baseball field.

Past the old teen-age hot spot, the Chesterland Hullabaloo, which today is a furniture store.

It was a splendid day. Sunny and warm. A day George Letts never saw.

George Letts, they said, had died. Died in an adopted town in southern Ohio. Heart problem. A surgery, an infection. Age 44.

George Letts was the fastest runner in my high school. He was thin and healthy, clean-cut and proper. National Honor Society. Football captain. Student Council. Homecoming court. Concert Band.

Later, a top private college (Kenyon). A good career. Kids.

Dead.

Same age as mine. Now, how can that be?

How did letter-sweaters and flirting with cheerleaders turn into doctors and catheters and a little patch of ground in a graveyard far from home?

George Letts attended the first reunion, the 10th, looking good. Talking about the "old days." About shared experiences, those bridges that carried us from elementary school to rookie adulthood. About how much fun it was to cross them and how much different the view looked from the other side.

That reunion was the last time I saw him.

I've lost several pals through car accidents, but never anything like this. Never anything connected with aging.

George Letts grew up on Sherman Road. It was the street of dreams for the West Geauga Class of 1970—not because George lived there, but because it was the unofficial summertime hangout for people with raging hormones and newly minted driver's licenses.

Back then, Sherman was a long, dusty, rural road, straight and flat. You could see the cops coming from a long way off. There was time to hide beer cans, to turn down the music, to button buttons.

Today, as a parent, I'm not at all sure I would approve of Sherman Road. Too much danger.

But in those days, Sherman Road was life itself. That glorious country trail was full of great, intense, important, exciting mysteries, mysteries just waiting for us to solve. Mysteries nobody else had ever solved.

Everybody has a Sherman Road. Your town doesn't matter.

This spring, George Letts drove through the dust of his Sherman Road for the last time. He took his childhood gleam, his grown-up dreams, his heart and his soul. He took it all and went away.

What he knew of me is gone, too. And, maybe, when we really think about it, that's what bothers us the most about an acquaintance passing on. When people we know go away, something of what makes us ourselves goes away, too. A mirror is broken.

When you reach a locale that no kid ever dreams he will actually reach—middle age—and things like this start to happen, it can feel as if you're sitting next to a glorious lake on a warm, clear evening, and the sun is setting, and the view is marvelous, and a heron is flying overhead, and everything is perfect, and you want to share it, but you look around and see that the people next to you have left. The folks who were beside you during the magical days of your youth have moved farther and farther away. And they're not coming back.

I lost touch with George Letts over the years, so I can't say for certain how he viewed the world upon reaching what was supposed to have been his halfway point. I hope he thought about the fragility of life and lived his accordingly. I'm pretty sure he did, because he always seemed to be doing the right thing.

But this time George Letts did the wrong thing. He died.

George Letts wasn't supposed to die. High school heroes don't die.

Some malicious little twerp hacked into God's computer and screwed up George Letts' script. And now I'm not sure how anybody else's story is going to turn out, either.

All I know is that the stories in that computer seem a lot shorter than they did before.

July 17, 1996

Not All There at E.J. Thomas

Akron's TubaChristmas gets better every year. Saturday's two-show spectacular at E.J. Thomas Hall drew a remarkable 5,600 people.

My family attended the second performance, and I wound up sitting next to a girl of perhaps age 10. On her other side was a younger sister. Next to the sister was their father.

I couldn't tell whether the girl next to me was enjoying herself, because she wasn't really there. She spent the entire 70-minute show sending and receiving text messages.

I don't mean she picked up her cell phone from time to time. I mean she used it constantly.

Not a single Christmas carol went by that she wasn't working her little keyboard, thumbs flying, her face illuminated by the light of the display.

Yes, it was annoying, and the father was remiss in not confiscating the phone. But it was less annoying than sad.

The episode reminded me that, as we keep developing more and faster ways of communicating, we're experiencing less and less of what's right in front of us.

Instead of living in the moment, letting the music and the atmosphere wash over her, the little girl was virtually MIA.

It's no secret that the pace of life keeps speeding up. A movie from 25 years ago seems to be playing in slow motion. A movie from 45 years ago is a still-life painting.

Back in 2000, I read (and wrote about) a great book called *Faster: The Acceleration of Just About Everything.* In it, author James Gleick noted that not much more than 200 years ago, fewer than 10 percent of the American public owned a watch. And not much more than 100 years ago, almost every town had its own time.

Time zones were invented by the railroad companies in 1883, when travel got fast enough to cause problems with the patchwork of local times. Until then, "noon" was when the sun was the highest over your immediate area—a difference of about 12 minutes between Akron and Pittsburgh.

Gleick also pointed out that many of the "timesaving" devices we keep inventing haven't saved us much time. Research shows that using a dishwasher—by the time you scrape, load and unload—cuts the task by about one minute.

Noted Gleick: "Some of us say we want to save time when really we just want to do more. To leave time free, it is necessary to decide to leave time free."

Most of us don't. We leap frantically from one thing to another for no apparent reason.

Reflection and introspection have nearly flat-lined.

Even at the age of 10, your days are numbered. Not a single person reading this will ever get today back again.

So this holiday season, let's try to slow down a little. Let's consider what we have. Let's remind ourselves that this could be the last Christmas for someone we love. Let's live in the moment—and in the room.

Dec. 23, 2010

Mogadore Rallies Behind Favorite Son

This is not a one-way relationship, this small-town love affair.

The people who exchange "high fives" with Ritchie Stefan get just as big a kick out of it as he does. Every time.

If Ritchie knows your name, you're somebody. And if you've met him once, he knows your name.

If Ritchie has seen your license plate, he knows that, too. His memory is epic.

"When we were children," says his younger brother, Roger, "we used to call him the Rolling Road Map.

"He was like the original Garmin. If we went somewhere once, he would get you there every time for the rest of your life."

Ritchie mostly walks places. And when you see him on the street, and you honk your horn, you will invariably get back a big wave and a bigger smile.

Ritchie Stefan has been giving and getting for most of the 41 years he has lived in the quiet village of Mogadore, one of the most tightly knit communities you'll ever find.

He is classified as high-functioning autistic. Friends compare him to the Dustin Hoffman character in *Rain Man*. Ritchie doesn't drive or do some of the other things most folks do, but what he does, he does very, very well.

Obsessively, you might say.

He's the first person at the high school football games and the last to leave. He goes to more basketball games than the coaches. In the 2011 *Beacon's Best* reader poll, Ritchie was voted the third-best "Hometown Fan" in the five-county region.

You can spot him in the local taverns, too, where he'll wear out the video games and, on karaoke nights, belt out Sinatra songs.

Ritchie pours his heart into everything he does—including the job he has held for 18 years at the Speedway gas station in the center of town.

A customer will walk into Ritchie's station, a customer Ritchie has known for decades—someone he knows so well that they exchange small talk about relatives and friends—and if that guy wants to buy a six-pack, Ritchie will card him. That's what he is supposed to do, so that's what he does. Simple as that.

If a customer presents a worn debit card that can't be read by the scanner, Ritchie will loudly proclaim, "Declined!" He'll try it again with the same result, and again bellow, "Declined!" The customer will laugh and pull out cash.

Everyone who has encountered Ritchie says he's good at his job—with one monumental exception.

On the first day of this month, Ritchie ran into a customer who was not pleased.

Justin McHenry, 28, has accused Ritchie of biting his hand, and has the photos to prove it.

McHenry says the bite was so severe that he had to get a tetanus shot and blood work to rule out such things as HIV. And when Ritchie's employer didn't immediately accede to McHenry's demand to cover his medical bills, McHenry started raising hell.

Ritchie's chomp was caught on the store's security camera. Unfortunately, the videotape did not include sound. So, with proof only that Ritchie bit McHenry, Speedway was in a bind. The corporation fired Ritchie two days later.

His fellow employees literally wept.

The whole town emotionally exploded. In one week, a Facebook page called "We Want Ritchie" had 1,583 members.

A big hand-painted sign was posted on the wall of a brick building directly across the street from the station that read: "RITCHIE—We are here for you."

Petition drives began. T-shirts were sold. Boycotts were urged. Dates were set for marches and picketing.

Late Thursday, shortly before the full frenzy of the town was unleashed, Speedway relented. Ritchie was rehired, with the same pay and benefits, plus back pay for his week in exile. He reported at 10 o'clock Friday morning.

It's not hard to guess why Speedway caved.

Mogadore police Chief Dave Fowler, who grew up in this village of 4,054 and has lived here for 35 of his 65 years, says, "I've never seen this town uprise like they have over the termination of Ritchie."

Speedway officials declined to talk about the situation, but clearly the station suffered a blow to the wallet.

"People have boycotted the station," Fowler said Friday. "I work during the day and I'm through the square probably 20 times. Usually, that place is packed at every pump. But even with gas prices down like they are, it's been pretty much a ghost town."

As word spread over the weekend that Ritchie had been rehired, customers started flocking back. Today, all is right with the world.

Well, almost all. Mr. McHenry is now widely considered a pariah, a guy who personifies the modern-day bully. He is taunted by strangers and threatened on Facebook.

McHenry says he served in the Marines, and, with two developmentally disabled stepbrothers, would never pick on someone like Ritchie.

A 2001 graduate of Garfield High, he has lived in Mogadore less than a year, in a house he rents from his parents, and says he literally doesn't know a soul. He works in Akron and his girlfriend lives there, so he has no local ties. But he stops at the Speedway all the time because "it's the only gas station in town."

McHenry flatly denies accusations that he provoked Ritchie or that the dispute had anything to do with him wanting to buy beer without an ID. He says he asked for a frozen Coke when Ritchie suddenly reached out, grabbed his hand and bit it.

Those who know Ritchie say that's absurd, something completely out of character—a character that has been in full public view for decades.

Asked to explain why Ritchie would suddenly do such a thing, McHenry said the two of them got off on the wrong foot awhile back when McHenry paid a bill using only coins.

Since then, McHenry says, Ritchie has greeted him by saying, "Here comes trouble."

McHenry points out that he refused to file charges and says all he wants is for Speedway to pay his medical bills.

"Unfortunately," he says, "uninformed people are making a big deal out of this."

A big deal it most certainly became.

Some residents lashed out angrily at both McHenry and Speedway (even though Speedway's local bosses weren't calling the shots).

The Springfield News-Sun reported Friday that the Dayton Bomb Squad had to detonate a suspicious package Thursday morning outside of Speedway's corporate headquarters in Springfield.

Company spokesman Shane Pochard (who would not permit Beacon Journal photographers to take Ritchie's photo when he returned to work) said he is not certain whether any connection exists between the bomb scare and the dispute in Mogadore, but "we don't believe so."

Mogadore's police chief isn't certain, either, but he says a link between the two would not surprise him in the least.

The situation was so volatile that the chief made certain an announcement about Ritchie's rehiring was read over the P.A. system at school Friday morning before a march on the gas station planned for that afternoon.

The fact the whole town had Ritchie's back comes as no surprise to brother Roger.

Twenty years ago, when Ritchie first started going to the Frosted Mug tavern, Roger swung by one day to check on him because Ritchie hadn't been out much on his own.

Roger walked in and approached Ritchie at the bar, where he was sipping a soft drink, and put his arm around him. Then, recalls Roger, "I looked up and everybody in the bar was staring right at me.

"I said, 'This is my brother.' Fortunately, he said, 'Yeah, this is my brother, Roger.' Then everyone went back to their business. I went home and said, 'You don't have to worry about him.' "

If Speedway had not seen the light, Ritchie would have had no trouble finding another job. Shortly after he was fired, Ron Hotchkiss, owner of the Avenue Market & Deli near the station, sent word to Ritchie's family he would love to hire him.

That marked the second time Hotchkiss had made a run at the town's most popular person. When the deli owner was preparing to launch his business, he tried to lure Ritchie away, but "he was too loyal to Speedway."

Ritchie is thrilled to be back at the modern, eight-pump station at Cleveland Avenue and state Route 532, just around the corner from the house where he lives with his mother and grandmother.

Still, last week was a long one for him. It took Ritchie awhile to process exactly what was happening, but he knew it wasn't good. He kept asking his mother, "I'm not going to jail, am I?"

With the situation resolved, his family is hoping that proceeds from the $15 "Team Ritchie" T-shirts will be donated to the Mogadore school district's anti-bullying initiative.

Meanwhile, Ritchie can go back to being Ritchie, which is all the residents of Mogadore ever wanted.

May 15, 2012

Wooster's Ernie Infield Leaves Lasting Legacy

I was livid.

It was a Saturday night, and all of my friends were partying on the other side of campus.

I had thought I was only a minute or two from joining them. But now my stupid boss was telling me I had to perform yet another task, a task I was sure could wait until Monday.

After graduating the previous year, I was an intern in the public-relations office at the College of Wooster, earning the princely sum of $4,000 for nine months of hard work. I was nearly fed up. It was morning, noon and night, weekdays and weekends.

I took photos and wrote stories about students and professors for campus publications, for students' hometown newspapers and for the local paper, the Wooster Daily Record.

Sports coverage was a big part of it, not only writing stories but also putting together media guides and game programs and keeping statistics.

My boss was the aptly named Ernie Infield.

Ernie died Saturday at the age of 89. He was a good man, and I will miss him.

Ernie Infield was a workaholic and a perfectionist at a time in my life when I was anything but. Not too many years after I escaped his clutches, I realized he was anything but a "stupid" boss. He was exactly what I needed at that time. He cared about me as a person. And nobody—before or since—taught me more about the craft of writing.

Ernest S. Infield didn't even have a four-year degree, but he could write circles around English professors. And unlike a lot of bosses responsible for cleaning up the work of inexperienced writers, he didn't just fix things; he sat you down and told you what he was fixing and why.

A track meet was a "dual" meet, not a "duel" meet—unless the coaches had introduced some type of high-stakes event of which he was unaware.

Someone scored "more than" 1,000 points in his basketball career, not "over" 1,000 points.

Try not to start a sentence with, "There were . . . " because that lifeless phrase makes the eyes glaze over. Give it some action, some drive.

To the college kids who worked under him, Ernie seemed more than a bit eccentric. He had a flat-top haircut and a military bearing when the popularity of both were at an all-time low. His passions were bird hunting and collecting baseball memorabilia.

And although his writing was technically superb, it could be incredibly corny, especially when he was coming up with walk-off lines for his "Ramblin' Round the Infield" column, a Daily Record fixture that began before I was born and continued long after I left town.

Ernie knew he was corny. In fact, he was proud of it. What counted, to him, was that his words were memorable.

Ernie's tutoring went far beyond writing. His primary mission, in retrospect, was teaching his charges how to function in the world of work.

He told us to shave every day, to dress decently and to show up on time.

He told us never to paper-clip something important to something else; always use a stapler, because stapled items are far less likely to become separated. He said he learned that lesson the hard way during his days as a successful sales manager, a career he left when a major heart attack signaled him to slow down.

Most of all, the taskmaster attempted to imbue young derelicts like me with a strong work ethic.

"If you're coasting," he was fond of saying, "you're going downhill."

Ernie Infield never coasted. He never took short cuts. And because of that, literally scores of young people who came through his office were less inclined to, either.

He was a lifelong organizer and innovator. As a Marine in the Pacific during World War II, he formed a regimental baseball league and wound up playing with and against such big-leaguers as Joe DiMaggio, Joe Gordon and Schoolboy Rowe.

Back home in Wayne County, he helped create an independent basketball league and start a local Hot Stove League. Arriving at the college in 1968, he formed a basketball booster group called the Downtown Rebounders, pulling together town and gown during an era when a lot of towns and a lot of gowns were at each other's throats.

He kept innovating long after his 1977 retirement, creating the Hank Critchfield Award, which he personally presented each year to the best defensive football player in the North Coast Athletic Conference. He named it after a 1927 Wooster graduate who founded a high-profile law firm.

Ernie knew all of the big shots, both in and out of sports. He was networking long before the term was coined, and his tentacles ran all over town and often far beyond.

Those connections helped his students land jobs in any number of fields. And when they did, they were prepared.

But Ernie . . . I mean really. Did you die on a Saturday just so I'd have to write this on a Sunday?

Aw, that's OK. I probably needed a refresher course.

Thank you, Ernie. Thanks for caring enough to make me mad.

March 30, 2009

A Walk In The Park is as Good as it Gets

I've gotten a bit jaded about vacations. If it doesn't include a beach, a pool, a luxury condo, boats, booze and wall-to-wall sun, I'm generally not interested.

So imagine my surprise when I discovered a vacation paradise right here in Akron. In November, no less.

What makes me think you'd be interested in how I spent my November vacation? Only that, on the eve of Thanksgiving, it may serve as a reminder that some of life's best moments are the ones that are the least choreographed and the most basic.

The fabulous vacation day in question cost me all of seven bucks.

With my 6 year-old in school and my wife Christmas shopping, I took my 4-year-old out to lunch, just to get out of the house.

First, Kimmie and I drove down to the Merriman Valley and went to McDonald's, the one with the giant tropical fish. We sat right in front of the main tank. A leisurely lunch? Let's put it this way: We stayed so long that we were on a first-name basis with the fish.

Kimmie named them. There was "Big Eyes," for obvious reasons. And "Bumpy," with ragged gills, "Rain" had vertical white markings. She talked about what the fish were thinking. She worried about the "shy" one who hid out in the rocks.

Finally we headed home via the big Smith Road hill. On a whim, we turned into Seiberling Naturealm. Odd day to visit a park. Cloudy, brisk, a Tuesday. Other folks had more sense: We saw only three people during the first five minutes, then not another soul for the next hour.

Kimmie helped me read the park map as we began our hike—our "ad-VEN-ture," as she called it.

Some adventure. Every five feet, she kept stopping, picking up acorns, knocking fungus off dead trees with her little walking stick. I found myself getting mildly irritated. I wanted to push on, to see where the trails led. Hey, the map shows another lake—let's find it!

But finally, the light bulb came on. I suddenly realized that Kimmie knew a lot more about using the park than I did.

It's about stopping, not charging ahead. It's about seeing what's right in front of you, not racing off over the next hill.

Soon I was helping her pick up acorns and knock "the fuzz" off dead trees. Whenever we decided to move on down the path, we took turns leading the way—hopping on one foot, walking backward, skipping.

We hung out with the chipmunks and squirrels. We poked our sticks into puddles of water that had welled up inside knots in trees. We made up stories.

She sounded out the letters in a "No Fishing" sign. Then she wondered whether the ducks on the pond were going to die someday.

"Everything dies eventually, honey."

"Even sticks?"

Got me on a technicality. "Only living things."

We talked gently about death, about relatives who had come before. She wanted to know if there was a heaven for ducks.

She seemed to give equal weight to the concept of death and to acorns. Just more factoids for her little organic computer.

Only later did I realize that part of the magic of my day came because I had spent it in the present tense. I wasn't fretting about what Kimmie might be like when she grew up, or what time we had to be home, or what I had to do the next day. We hung out until we were good and ready to move on.

I also realized I had right before me the best gift I would get this or any other holiday season: a healthy, bright, cute, inquisitive little girl who enjoys hanging out with Dad. The ultimate gift. And for once I was smart enough to cherish it—every word she spoke, every laugh, every little-kid question.

For a while, we froze time. She was 4. I was her undistracted father. We were buddies, out on an "ad-VEN-ture."

No matter what happens to either of us in the months and years to come, I will always have that cloudy afternoon in Akron.

Vacations just don't get any better than that.

Happy Thanksgiving.

Nov. 29, 1994